A Plan For You

By Deena Anderson Cardinale

Xulon
PRESS

Copyright © 2008 by Deena Anderson Cardinale

A Plan For You
by Deena Anderson Cardinale

Printed in the United States of America

ISBN 978-1-60791-079-4

All rights reserved solely by the author. The author guarantees all contents are original and do not infringe upon the legal rights of any other person or work. No part of this book may be reproduced in any form without the permission of the author. The views expressed in this book are not necessarily those of the publisher.

Unless otherwise indicated, Bible quotations are taken from The NIV. Copyright © 1978 by Zondervan Bible Publishers.

www.Sonshinewriter.com

www.xulonpress.com

A Plan For You

I chose you at birth
a mere babe crying in my arms –
Right from the start
I've had a plan for you
I watched you at play,
a little girl
jumping on my hand –
Right from the start
I've had a plan for you
I marveled at your growth,
a young lady
shining in my eyes –
Right from the start
I've had a plan for you
I celebrate your womanhood,
a spirit filled child
praising my name –
Right from the start
you're fulfilling my plan for you!

By Deena Anderson Cardinale

Dedication

My Dedication goes to God the Father, God the Son and God the Holy Spirit.
And to my Daddy Frank.

Introduction

And I lived happily ever after. I had no more problems, no more heartache, and no more hard days. I got my life aligned with Jesus and all was perfect. "Lalalalala."

There was no doubt that my faith was stronger and I interacted with God more through my deep heartaches. And the close encounters that my daughter, Marcie and I had with Him during her illness and following her death were miraculous.

I was blest. I was more connected to Jesus. But as a human, I was weak in the flesh. I'd often set Him aside to live my life the way I desired; which I knew wasn't very pleasing to Him. But Jesus was faithful and just to forgive me, over and over again. He knew I'd get through the sin-barriers and the storms to see the undying, unconditional love He had for me. Unbeknownst to me, my many connections with Jesus, beginning from my childhood, were moving me toward a permanent and firm foundation. I was chosen for a purpose; His plan for my life on earth was in miraculous making.

A Plan For You

Jeremiah 29:11- For I know the plans I have for you, plans to prosper you and not to harm you, plans to give you hope and a future.

Lingering Grief

Chapter 1

"Nurse, please don't let that baby die," I begged. Tears streamed down my cheeks as I lay on the cot in the emergency room. The crying baby pierced my soul. I knew without a doubt that children do die, and I hadn't been in a hospital for exactly one year to the date – May 22$^{nd.}$ The date my 9 year old daughter, Marcie died of cancer.

That day I wasn't myself; I hadn't been myself all year. I was in a numb state. The morning meeting at my workplace seemed to set off dormant emotions. There was talk about a man coming into the Center who had cancer and was on chemo therapy treatment. As the social worker talked about the man I started feeling dizzy and sick to my stomach. I excused myself from the group and started walking to the room where there were some beds. I passed out, hit my head and wet my pants. When I came too, I cried uncontrollably. A coworker rushed me to the hospital emergency room.

As I listened to the baby cry, memories of Marcie encompassed my mind. She cried a lot her first few months of life because of colic. I wanted my baby back.

"Please doctor, take care of the baby," I sobbed. I explained to him about Marcie's death.

The doctor listened to my sad story, realizing the symptoms were grief-related. There was no medical cure. The time lapse made Marcie's passing more final. She wasn't coming back.

The depression hit hard. I slept every moment that I could. I cried when I was awake. I forced myself to go to work. It was a real effort to tuck in my blouses and brush my hair – living was an effort.

My son, Jim was fending for himself. Something he was doing while Marcie was sick. He was worried. He didn't know how to deal with my deep grief, and neither did I.

My parents were too far away, and Jim thought I needed someone close enough to get me out of bed, so he called Brandy and asked for her help. Brandy remained my faithful friend, as did Will, his mother and his family.

Although, for some, it may have seemed awkward that Will and Brandy married, but we had been in the same circle of friends for five years. And really, having a relationship was no longer forefront in my life. I was a young woman and still desired attention from a man, but my children and God (to a certain extent) had taken more of center stage. Jim was taking a back seat to Marcie again, and so was Jack.

A Plan For You

I was still dating Jack, but he most definitely didn't know how to deal with my sadness. His lack of faith in God didn't help matters. His in-sensitive comments for me to toughen up placed a tinge of hidden anger in me: "Don't cry; you have to be strong." That was easy for "Mr. Control of emotions" to say. It wasn't his little girl.

I was in the heart of my grief. I stayed away from him more because of his lack of understanding. Plus, he had this self need for me to behave like the perfect lady, and to only hang around people he approved of.

I'm not going to say that Jack was heartless, he had many good qualities. He worked hard, set goals, climbed the corporate ladder, and got what material things he wanted in life. It was his down fall to be such an image setter; and then it didn't help matters that he wasn't sharing his goals with me. He may have thought about sharing his life outside of the convenient way it was – I live here and you live there. But the convenient way really wasn't motivating our relationship.

I chose to dress, hang out with, and behave the only way I knew how. I will admit to not always behaving like a perfect lady. One incident comes to mind. Jack had invited some friends over to his house to play pool. I didn't drink much, so when I did, I got buzzed quickly. I got loud and laughed obnoxiously. I was the only one having fun, I guess. I made the perfect fool of myself. Add this episode and his lack of understanding and nurturing to my sensitive self and this would soon equal: Audios Amigo.

Brandy was attentive to our friendship, and she was quite interested in aiding to my sensitive self that was suffering at a maxed out level.

I was behaving rather strangely, as Jim had explained to her. "Mom sleeps all the time and she ain't eatin'; can you help her?"

Receiving that call from Jim worried Brandy. She was at my side immediately, even though, she lived one hour away. She pretty much forced me out of the house. If a person desired to see a lot of the world in a day, Brandy would be the best friend for the job. Try as she might, she couldn't get me pass the deep blues. No one could.

It was obvious to my coworkers that something wasn't right; after all, I was taken to the emergency room from my workplace. They were all aware of Marcie's death a year prior. Being a multi-disciplinary staff of nurses, social workers, and occupational therapists, they were somewhat equipped to help me through my misery.

People would attempt to show their comfort and concern, but none could muster up enough to change my dying spirit. I missed Marcie so much, and the thought of not having her around anymore – I couldn't stand it.

Several dark weeks engulfed me, suffocating the life out of me. I was growing accustomed to the heaviness. Sleep was the best way to escape.

One afternoon, I was awoken by the bright sunlight shining through the window. My eyes opened, and I stared at the ceiling. The tears surged. "God, please let me go back to sleep." But words came back to

A Plan For You

me: "Get out of bed. I would never want you to feel this sad. Jim needs you now." It was God's way of speaking to me, but I could hear Marcie.

Those words penetrated my mind, as I sat on the edge of my bed. A smile came to my face. "Thank you, Father." I stayed in a euphoric state of mind for a while.

Through God, Marcie was letting me know that is was good to go on with my life and to be there for Jim.

Marcie in her infinite wisdom knew I would have hard days on earth. "God prays for you to get through your hard days." She wrote these words on an Easter card that she had made for me one month before she went home with Jesus.

Romans 8:26 – In the same way, the Spirit helps us in our weakness. We do not know what we ought to pray, but the Spirit Himself intercedes for us with groans that words cannot express.

It was these words that helped me get through the most painful time of my life. This verse would be there to remind me of just how much Jesus loves me and cares about my pain on earth during more hard days and challenging circumstances straight up ahead.

Jim's Journey

Chapter 2

After Marcie's death, Jim and I were closely connected. Hearing the Lord's comforting words telling me that Jim needs me and Marcie wouldn't want me to be sad, placed my living child first in my life.

We did everything together: rode our bikes, went swimming and picnicking and jogged.

Although Marcie had no control over her physical condition and death, Jim and I became obsessed about keeping our bodies healthy. Jim was well aware what cancer could do. He watched it rapidly destroy his sister's body in a matter of five months.

It was hard for him to let her go. At her funeral, he wanted to know why she couldn't be in a glass casket so he could see her whenever he wanted. He had just turned 11 years old a month prior to Marcie dying. He apparently had no idea about decomposing, or chose not to believe this occurred; all he knew is he didn't want her body to go in the ground. It was too final that way.

I tried to explain to Jim that Marcie was already in heaven with Jesus. But the reality of seeing her dead body in front of him made it difficult for him to understand that truth.

He may have been living with his own guilt about praying for God to take her the same night she died. That was a big thing for a small boy to live with; even if I tried to convince him that he had nothing to do with the time God chose to take Marcie.

Jim's journey through the loss of Marcie wasn't as noticed by family and friends, as they were focused on me. And up until the words through God from Marcie came to me to get up and get on with my life, I wasn't paying attention to Jim's journey either.

He slept with her blanket and favorite stuffed dog. He wanted to stay close to her any way he could. He was living with fear, a reality that kids do die.

A few months following his sister's death, he had been picking strawberries with a friend, and after he ate some berries his friend told him that he could get cancer from the spray they used on the berries.

Jim had started getting migraines at 5 years old, it seemed school was a mental challenge for him. He did have difficulty learning in school and ended up in Special Ed, which was even more traumatizing. Kids can be cruel.

The more stress in his little life, the more headaches. His sister's death impacted his emotions and he had some intense migraines.

That day, while picking berries, he had one of his those headaches and was throwing up, so he was certain that he had cancer.

"Mom, I ate berries with poison. I've got cancer. I gotta' go to the doctor."

I made an appointment that very day. The doctor had also been Marcie's Pediatrician. I reminded him of Jim's headaches, and he already knew why he was so fearful of cancer. So the doctor went through a thorough examination and reassured Jim in between each test, "I can't find any sign of cancer. You just have a bad headache." He was a perfect Pediatrician. He convinced Jim that he was healthy, gave us some medicine for his headaches and the examination was free. He may have convinced him, but I'm sure he continued to have his own secret fears.

If we were obsessed about our health, we were certainly having fun in the process.

One thing that Jim and I had in common was our hyperactivity. We channeled this energy into physical activity. Jim took karate, wrestling, bicycling and running, and I was into exercising, dancing, bicycling and jogging. Plus I gave up smoking for Marcie and Jim. Marcie often asked me to quit, and I figured if I couldn't give the bad habit up for a dying child, then something was really wrong with me.

Having a healthy body and active life was a good way to sustain my physical health, but it didn't prevent the spells of darkness from hitting me so hard at times I had difficulty seeing a glimpse of light.

Thrill Seeking

Chapter 3

Adventurous living had become my focal point. Jim and I were having fun for the most part. But I was also doing things to bury the pain. Losing a child is an endless grieving process. And having a violent screwed up childhood didn't go away over night.

I searched for things that would be a challenge, and that I could accomplish.

I received a flyer in the mail for free belly dance lessons, and I went for it like the dancing maniac that I was. I found this to be an exciting new challenge. I had become a goal seeker - okay, a thrill seeker. I viewed this style dance as an art. It took years to become an accomplished dancer; let alone, create all those beautiful costumes. Nope, a person doesn't just step on stage and perform this art form instantaneously.

Exercising, jogging, bicycling and dancing, weren't enough to fulfill me; I needed something even more thrilling to feed my adventurous spirit.

A Plan For You

I'm not sure how I got enthused about Sky Diving, but I had a strong desire to jump from a perfectly good airplane. This was as close to flying like Superman as I could get. Riding on a Harley-Davidson was just as thrilling in comparison to jumping in the sky.

I learned where to go to jump, and after I was given six hours of ground training, up in the plane I went. The instructions were clear: when the Instructor says jump – you jump. Otherwise you may land in a place you don't want to – like water, the highway, or a tree.

"Okay, knees to the breeze. "

I moved to the open door of the plane and dangled my feet in the air. I can't remember what thoughts were going through my mind, as I knew I was seconds away from jumping into the air.

"Are you scared?"

"Yea, I am."

"You wouldn't be doing this if it wasn't scary."

The Instructor was right about that; that was the point, I was defying death or life, depends on how one wants to observe it. I was seeking excitement in life that would thrill me or kill me. Some of what I did was for burying pain, and much of what I did was for the purpose of bringing pleasure and attention to me (Me, Me, and Me). I was actively contending with the ME virus.

Common Threads

Chapter 4

I believe Jesus made no mistakes when he gifted me with friends. As well as, Brandy, my English friend, Marty and I were still close.

It seemed as though the beginning of the '80's was the season for relationship endings. Brandy and Will's marriage didn't last long; Marty's husband packed up and left her one day while she was at work; and my relationship with Jack didn't survive for obvious reasons. And my new neighbor was stirring up the neighborhood over her cheating man.

Shortly after Marcie died, we moved into a town house that was located directly across the street from my job. It may have been best to move out of the house that had strong reminders of her life and death.

JoDee reminded me of me a few years earlier. I was drawn to her like she was a sister. She was nine years younger than me and fighting her man the same way I did when I was fighting men

A Plan For You

in my twenties. She had two little girls. JoDee had strawberry blond hair and hazel eyes. She was shorter than me. But when it came to taking on a cheating man, she was big and bad.

One evening JoDee and her boyfriend were at a small gathering at our neighbor Bill's place for a party. Bill was a gentle man and my buddy. We did many fun things together and he was fond of Jim as well. Jim would become his guinea pig, as he was going to hygienist school. That was an experience Jim has never forgotten. Yes, I could have men friends on rare occasions. I trusted Bill and he was my friend, although he didn't know Jesus. There wasn't too much connecting us, except his strong interest in my son.

But several men in my life weren't trustworthy, and my friend, JoDee was about to experience her long term relationship wasn't based on trust, but on lust.

JoDee had left early and when much time passed, she went back over and was shocked to find him in bed with a young gal.

I was woken out of my dead sleep. Her voice shrilled out harsh words that were meant to verbally kill him (stimulating my memory of times I was cursing men in my past). I looked out my window to see clothes being thrown out of JoDee's bedroom window. She had cut them up with a large knife before throwing them at the cheating boyfriend. He was brave or stupid, as he came inside to a raging woman. She swung the knife back and forth in front of him threatening to stab him.

And a year later, they were having a physical confrontation. He had her by the throat, attempting to choke her. She couldn't breathe. She felt that she was struggling for her life. There were knives on the kitchen counter, she managed to grab one and stabbed him in the arm. After that, the man never laid a hand on her again, and their relationship was over.

JoDee could have fit right into my family. Being fighters was what my siblings and I had become as a result of living through Dad's abuse and violence.

Family Resemblance

Chapter 5

Yes, JoDee's temperament would have fit right in the family. My sister, Sherry was sharp with the tongue. She could go for the juggler and kill a person's spirit with her words. Sister, Stormy was a defense fist fighter and her victims were usually men. Brother, Mark was scary as he enjoyed pain and torture, and found this to be funny.

I was in the justice business, and I was the jury who went right past the verdict and gave them their due punishment.

We were all examples of "Children live what they learn."

How did Mom live with such a restless bunch of kids? And what a patient man, Daddy Frank was. He married Mom when my siblings were approaching adolescence, and I had just become a teen. We seemed to get rougher with age. And he was a saint to except and love us.

Family Fighting

"It's your turn to warsh the broiler pan; ya' let it soak long enough," Stormy yelled at Sherry.

"You're doin' the dishes; you can warsh it," Sherry responded, as she walked to the bathroom. Stormy followed quickly behind. They began shoving one another. And "poof" there I was in the middle of their fight.

In the meantime, Mark had invited one of our new neighbors over. We hadn't lived in the neighborhood long, and this neighbor was about to get the welcome he would never forget.

Sherry and I fought from one end of the house to the other, yelling, hair pulling, shoving, pinching, and biting. Sherry was going for my juggler, working on killing me with words, reminding me of every flaw I had and working hard to convince me that I was stupid. And actually, her words would penetrate the way Dad's did when he called me dumb blank and other harmful names. We worked our way out to the family room where Mark and his friend were watching us; Mark was cheering us on, enjoying the fighting. We kept it up until Mom finally broke us up. Mom spent a good portion of our youthful years braking up fights.

My brother's new friend spread the news to all the other new neighbors, giving us a bad standing in the neighborhood; that is, until they realized we weren't in the habit of beating other people up that often, and we could be quite fun to be around.

A Plan For You

Sherry was strong at verbally hurting her opponent. She learned how to kill with words at a very young age and this aggressive skill grew better with age. Being Daddy's girl had obligations to obtain, in order to hold her title of top child. Add that to a group of jealous siblings and her hidden anger and a vicious mouth retaliated.

Boxing Match

There was no getting around the rough life-style; it seemed to be inbred. My brother did occasionally get into fist fights with some of his friends. But when he was 14 years old he got a pair of boxing gloves for Christmas. He always wanted to box with someone, and that usually ended up being his sisters.

When I boxed with Mark, he didn't show any mercy on me, so I had to punch back hard. Then it turned into a real match. This was exactly what he wanted to happen. He laughed at his every punch and that would make me mad, and I'd hit him even harder.

I stopped boxing with him, but then he had another game that he talked me into playing: Punch out.

That game had a rule. You can only punch in the arm. The first one to give in loses. I gave it my best shot, but I lost. My arm turned black and blue, but so did his.

It may have been innocent fun in his eyes as a teen, but unfortunately, my brother was already taking drugs and drinking alcohol. Alcohol became his drug of choice as an adult. This seemed to intensify his need to fight and hurt people. It was as though he was paying people back for his abuse that he lived through as a child. Although we were all whipped, slapped, punched and called names, he was physically and verbally picked on the most, and he became violent just like our Dad.

Defense Fighter

Stormy grew stronger at defending herself in her teen years, but her fighting went overboard. She'd outright take on grown men without blinking an eye when it came to defending anyone that she loved.

One night we three sisters and Stormy's first husband, Jake went out to Sherry's boyfriend's club. Jake was a little guy with a big mouth. He was mouthing off to some guy in the pool room. Stormy, Sherry and I sat at the bar talking to Gene, Sherry's boyfriend.

The mad man retaliated Jake's words by punching and shoving him. Stormy jumped from the bar stool and started punching and pinching and cursing at the man to leave her husband alone. The bouncer stepped in to throw Jake out of the bar; Jake attempted to fight the bouncer back. The bouncer began getting too rough for Stormy's liking, so she punched him over and over and then dug at his eyes with her long fingernails. My sisters and I decided that we should take Jake home. But I couldn't find my car; I didn't remember where I parked it – oh those were the days I'd rather forget.

A Plan For You

The bouncer later made comments about staying clear of Stormy, that she was scary. And yes, she was. Shortly after I moved to Seattle, another man would get into her defensive wrath. She shoved him off a balcony. He lived not to mess with her or her people ever again. Stormy was even keeled until you messed with her people.

To hide her abusive childhood, she chose to become oblivious and ignored the facts, but aggression came out of her when someone was hurting someone she loved.

Justice Fighter

My brother had some of the guys over to our small run down home – the home where a lot of Dad's violent episodes occurred. Dad was gone and Mom was dating Daddy Frank then. I was just coming into puberty. I was a sucker for wanting the attention of these boys. They were the popular boys in school. For some reason they wanted me to do jumping jacks for them. I was so stupid. I thought there was some good reason behind why they wanted me to jump for them. After all, I was very athletic. As I dramatically did the jumping jacks, they began laughing at me.

"Yep, she's got hair under her arms," one said, pointing. They continued to laugh louder.

I was so hurt and embarrassed; tears welled in my eyes, as I ran into the little house. I pulled out the largest butcher knife I could find from the silverware drawer. I came back out of the house where the boys stood having a hay day over my underarm hair.

"I'm gonna' kill all of ya'" I yelled, as I lunged toward them. The shocked boys ran down the street like they had just seen a monster – and it was the raged monster in me.

I grew up wanting to hurt people back for hurting me – namely men. I responded violently when I was jealous, I didn't know any other way to respond. Dad was a rage of a man when he was jealous. Although much of his jealousy wasn't justified. My response to being hurt unduly was all about justice.

I also hated to see people bullied. I interrupted a few unfair fist fights in the back of the high school, or outside a night club. If the fight was unfair in anyway and the victim was unable to defend himself (down on the ground being punched and kicked) there I was, right in the middle.

I'd get right in the bully's face, place my hands on my hips (there was something about my hands on my hips that implicated that I was in complete control, and that I wouldn't take any crap from anyone.

I was lucky that no one ever retaliated when I interrupted their fights. As a result I saved a few guys butts and grew up expecting justice.

I grew to want to stop others from getting hurt. I was helpless to prevent it from occurring in my household as a girl, but I wasn't going to put up with it as a grown up. If I got hurt, I hurt back; if I witnessed someone hurt someone unjustly, I'd interrupt the perpetrator. If only I could have done something to keep our perpetrator from causing so much damage in my house.

But I wasn't able to stop our perpetrator, and there was another life fight I didn't know how to battle, and that was, the verbal controlling or under minding of my character, making me feel I shouldn't have been born. I'd run away from it, if at all possible. That's the only way I knew how to deal with it as a child. Dad's sick control over my body, mind and emotions left a deep scar that cut the center of my self esteem. Living with such intense abuse does not dissipate, as I've mentioned before.

These stories may have a funny overtone, but the undertone has a terrible affect on all of us in our adult years. And so it can be said that not only does physical and sexual abuse hurt, so do words.

Attention Addiction

Chapter 6

Being a young woman in my early thirties, I was still interested in having a relationship.

I was a weak human vessel, living in the world; therefore, I responded to its calling. I was a sucker for the undivided attention of a man. I had a lingering low self esteem where men were concerned. Unfortunately, this kept me from overlooking sin, and making excuses up for what I knew deep inside was not right.

Mike was the best man for this undivided attention addiction. He was a dark haired man with dark eyes. He was a tender man, and appeased a part of me no other man was able to do. He liked to sing and dance. He was open with his feelings, which is rare with many men. He was rebuilding his life after dealing with a troublesome past. He was going to college, learning skills in aircraft mechanics. And when he talked highly of God, this made it easier to overlook the things that were wrong about the relationship;

A Plan For You

that is, until Mike became involved in things that I did not believe or feel comfortable with. He was practicing and studying Trans something meditation and he joined a group that had an interesting concept about God. At first it sounded okay, after all, God was at the center of their belief.

Mike invited me to one of the group meetings. I sat in the group and felt okay at first, as they seemed to be a friendly bunch. They talked about God's forgiveness and that registered. Then a member came in late and started saying she could see the glowing light around the others – the ora thing, leaving me out of whatever she was seeing. Suddenly, I felt a little uneasy. But I continued to listen.

Then the teacher went on with his lesson about Jesus being God; okay that's good, I thought. But then he threw me off course, when he said, "Jesus is God and being that He is, He was not capable of feeling pain."

That did it! I became defensive and blurted out, "What do you mean He felt no pain? He was nailed to the cross and He was beat and bled! Now tell me how that didn't hurt?"

He went on to try and explain his theory of why Jesus could not feel pain; it was way out there, as far as I was concerned.

"No, my Bible says He was hurt big time; He was in a lot of pain hangin' on that cross to pay for our sins!"

Then I took notice of the people surrounding me, and I felt as though I was in a bad dream, as though I had taken a hit of acid and was hallucinating;

although I was sober. I'd seen this scene before in an unpleasant setting – a dejavue. I felt an evil presence in the room. The members piercing looks were saying they were quite unhappy with me. I strongly felt God speak to my heart telling me to get out of there.

I looked at Mike; he didn't appear scary to me nor did he seem too affected by my out bursts about their dumb logic. Most likely because he wasn't sucked in deep enough to their belief system.

I immediately stood up and whispered in Mike's ear, "These people are weird; they are freakin' me out. I'll wait for ya' in the car." He stayed for the rest of the meeting. He was fully aware that I was upset; after all, I was arguing with the leader. When he returned to me, I tried to explain the strange vision to him, and loudly voiced my knowledge of Jesus. "How can you believe that stuff they said about Jesus?"

Mike didn't argue with me, nor did he agree with me. He stayed rather calm as he responded, "What's so wrong with the way they believe?"

"You're crazy, how can ya' believe that junk! Jesus felt pain and he feels our pain now!"

I thought about Marcie's words again and the *Romans 8:26*. God cries and prays for us. The words of this verse came to my rescue in the midst of my deep grieving, and now as a defense mechanism to remind me of the truth: Jesus felt physical pain and still feels our pain. He was God's Son, born in the flesh. He was human while on earth. He experienced physical and mental pain. How else could he relate to humans?

A Plan For You

I tried to explain my biblical truth to Mike, but it appeared to go over his head. He didn't know Jesus the way I did. I was a believer with a certain amount of conviction; that much was fair to say.

"Please, let's not argue about it. You make a strong point. But I think there's more to God."

"You better be careful with that line of thinkin.'"

We drove home in silence. But my mind was not quiet. I was thinking about the intensity of the whole morning: the horrific encounter and the strange belief system. I had an overpowering need to read my Bible to search for more truth about Jesus.

I'm sure Mike believed some of what I told him of the image that I experienced; after all, he was meditating and worshipping some dead man that I had never heard of, and he seemed to believe what this group was teaching him. I felt as though Mike was getting more lost, and God was working hard to reel me in closer to Him.

I knew what I saw was real, as God had been showing me visions since I was a little girl, some heavenly, and some down right scary.

Because of that experience, I recognized strength in my faith. The Holy Spirit was implanted in my heart. I loved Jesus and would defend Him, and He had a high place in my life, but not high enough.

Flipping Through

Flipping through the pages
of life – of living
I come close to Jesus,
But not close enough
Flipping through His Word
of truth – of triumph
I come even closer,
but not close enough

Flipping Through

Chapter 7

After the strange encounter at the meeting I was drawn to read my rainbow pictured Bible, the one Mrs. Teshera had given me in Sunday school class when I was a girl. The legacy one, the same one Marcie spent time reading when she was sick. I wanted to prove to myself that I was right about my belief in Jesus. I really wanted to know the man that took Marcie to live with Him.

Two young Christians were in Mike's college class, which I felt was no coincidence. I enjoyed being around them. One of the young men, Richard, was a missionary. He was learning how to work on airplanes so that he could go back to Peru to do God's work. He would be flying, ministering and keeping the small aircrafts in working condition.

I enjoyed listening to him talk about Peru. But when he talked about the strange things ate (like monkey brains) my stomach did flip flops. But when in Peru, do as they do.

A Plan For You

I felt secure around these men and their wives. I envied them. I desired to have a strong man of God in my life. But a wee voice said, "You aren't good enough for someone like this;" plus, there was still an unresolved restlessness in me yet, that a Godly man couldn't reach. I was attracted to men that had enough bad in them, to keep my self - esteem from rising. God, in His faithful Wisdom, kept trying to raise me higher.

Richard gave me his old NIV Bible and I found it easy to read; it was like reading a regular book. I read Revelations to my son. He was 16 years old and was into scary. He liked hearing about all the creatures and disasters.

I avidly read it, even brought it with me to Mike's apartment.

Jesus was tugging on my heart, and Mike's unhealthy tenderness pulled me in his direction. Mike continued searching for God in his strange way. And even though his friends and I were Christians, he continued his strange practices. I did not let him influence my way of believing. But there was a definite strain.

So when Mike fell off the wagon, I had no problem leaving the affection behind.

I went to his apartment one morning to find him and one of his friends so drunk they couldn't even talk. They were staggering and falling down. The place smelt of stale beer. My heart didn't hurt. I was sickened to my stomach - disgusted would be a better word. He was aware I was there. His slurring was hardly understandable. I looked into his red eyes and said absolutely nothing. I left, and as I drove away a euphoric free feeling came over me. I was glad it was over.

Braking off relationships was much easier to do since Will. I believe that stemmed from my bruised ego that my ex-husband, Wilson and Will left me with. They had played a big part in leaving scars, but the largest wounds came from my abusive father.

I liked being in control of whose leaving who. I had a mechanism implanted deep that would only let my affection for a man go so far; that way I would never be hurt. I did my share of crying in all of my relationships, thinking I needed them in my life, but I was getting better at letting them go when time presented itself. Love – what did I know? I was flipping through to find perfect love.

And while I searched and kept turning those pages, perfect love was trying to find me.

Inspiration

My Inner strength is so low
My spirit's without an even flow
I am filled with confusion, anger and pain
In my heart there's a stormy rain
I want to scream and be mean
I want to hide so I won't be seen
I want to cry
Far away to heaven I want to fly
I wish to receive God's assurance
for this overwhelming reoccurrence
God would let me know, I am really alright,
That I am always in His sight
God would wipe away my tears
and take away my fears
Being emotional is a special part of me
this my Lord wishes me to see
Emotions are necessary in growing
This is to keep me flowing
Pain and sorrow are a part of life
God feels my every strife
God loves me so very much
My heart, He longs to touch
With His love I will prevail
And away I will sail
I am God's special child so full of love
He watches over me carefully from above!

My Prayer

Please don't take the smile from my face
Please don't let the tears take its place
Forgive me for my anxious and hasty ways
Please replace them with patience and understanding
That will last for days and days
I pray not to be so concerned of what
Will partake in my life
I just don't need all of that strife
I know it is written that you know
my needs before I ask
So place this knowledge in my heart
and let if forever last
Please Father, won't you guide me,
your child
I know that you can make my life nice
and mild
Please be by my side
So my smile will remain ever so wide.

Crashing

Chapter 8

Not only was I more drawn to read the Bible, I was compelled to write poetry. I didn't know much about writing at the time, but I could sure rhyme and cry out to the Lord when I was in trouble. I had no idea where jotting down words on a piece of paper was going to take me. I got comfort from writing poems; especially when I felt depressed and hopeless; which would become a life pattern I wasn't able to unweave so easily.

Working in the Day Center for five years had given me a sense of confidence, in that, I felt important to the participants and I was constantly learning and growing. This was good for a sensitive young woman who had a lingering sensitive ego.

I held on to my job at the Day Center, as my self-indulged dream of becoming an accomplished belly dancer, and an aerobic instructor, teaching and running my own school, would become nothing but and off and on side job.

The staff and the participants appreciated my character and heart; I made more than a sufficient wage; I bought my first new car and I had spending money. Yes, life was rather good, until the crashing came to crumble my world.

Mary was a participant who had found comfort in being around me. We had developed a friendship in the five years I had been at that workplace. She got to my heart.

Mary was manic-depressive. She took pride in her appearance; her golden curls neatly combed and she always wore a dress. She was tall and thin and had erect posture. She was a perfect example of a lady. She was quiet by nature ... until her manic demons showed up.

There was no doubt when it was time to console and counsel Mary. She would come to the Center wearing pants, messy hair, and her blouse not tucked in. She'd smoke like a flaming forest fire with no end in sight. When not smoking, she would pace the halls like a nervous caged animal.

I was fully aware of her condition and was right there when the signs from hell arrived. She was on my case load, as I had a way of getting her to open up to me.

Through the years as I paced and walked with Mary, I had learned that her Minister father had caught her having sex when she was a teenager. Apparently it was an unforgivable sin, as her father and mother constantly reminded her that she was a whore and was going to hell. The trauma of this troubled time possessed Mary. She began to hear voices telling her she was a whore and to kill herself. She had been fighting this battle every since the tragic day she was caught in the sex act. It carried over through the years causing her husband and children to desert her because they didn't understand her illness.

I did my best to counteract her troubled spirit. I would remind her that Jesus loves and forgives her; that he would never want her to feel so guilty. And to be honest, I can't remember everything that I said to her, but I do feel that God was speaking through me to reach Mary. She'd always tell me she felt better when she talked to me; that I understood her. As strange as it may seem, I did understand.

I lived through some childhood trauma of my own, living with an evil dad. I even had the devil himself appear in my life as a little girl and again as a young woman, and he wasn't done with me just yet. I'd come to work disheveled myself when I was depressed and grieving over Marcie's death.

I loved Mary and I wanted her to accept God's love, enough to forgive herself (I could have applied this to myself at the time). I told her that it was a sin not to forgive, and that her family was wrong in not forgiving her.

I was approaching my fifth year at the Center when Mary's behavior intensified to the point that she could barely hear my voice. She came into work unkempt. I was immediately at her side. She grabbed my hand and pulled me into a restroom. She pointed at the wall and started crying. "Please take those chains off of Peter." I can't, Mary; I don't see Peter." She just kept weeping as we anxiously paced together.

A Plan For You

The family where she lived called to tell us she had gone out and laid in the road scraping her elbows and knees, waiting for a car to run over her.

She let me look at her wounds and I asked, "Mary, why did you hurt yourself?"

"The demons told me to kill myself."

No matter what I said to calm her, it wasn't happening. She was hypnotized – as though she were under a dark spell; essentially she was.

I talked with some of the staff. The social worker, Mack said she needs to go to the Gero-psych unit of the hospital. I was helpless to do anything for Mary.

I took her there, and then visited her the next day, she appeared even more disheveled. She was zombiefied because of the drugs the doctors prescribed for her. Mary's response to me wasn't but a few words. My heart ached for her. I was growing weary for my tormented friend.

I came into work the next day and Mack immediately came to my office. He said, "I have bad news. Mary drowned herself in a bathtub last night."

"No way; is this a joke?" I knew it wasn't, it just seemed so unreal. How was that possible, I thought? I knew Mary was haunted and desperate enough to do this, but no one could intentionally drown themselves, I never heard of this happening – ever.

"Where'd she do this?" I responded, as the tears were showing up.

"At the family home."

"She wasn't suppose to be home. She wasn't in any condition to go home. Why would they do that?" I said, raising my voice a few notches. Then the crying started. Mack was the best person to share the news. He had a big heart for Mary as well.

My friend, Pastor James was again around through another tragic death. He was still working on the grounds of the state hospital, of where our Day Center was connected. Mary and I sat in on his weekly services together for several years. This was my way of attending church. His sermons rubbed off enough keep me interested in God.

He was still the only pastor that I was involved with since Marcie's illness and death. I loved and respected him more than he was aware. There he was, pastor and comforter of another funeral, another tragedy in my life.

Mary's funeral was sad, as there were only a few people there, her family home members, and Mack and I. I was glad that I could be a strong part of her life – accepting and loving her. I was her family and I will meet her again, as I know God took her home with Him; for Mary loved and believed in Jesus, even in the midst of her terror. The demons did not win her soul.

Crumbling

Chapter 9

After going through Mary's horrific death, I fell into a depression. That was a shocking experience, and swallowing it wasn't going down easy. My boss, Jess told me that I had aged ten years. My co-workers supported me and counseled me. They understood the mental anguish I had endured. A few of them were there for me when Marcie died. Changes are constant in the caring business, and I worked with several new faces in my years at the Center.

I put my whole heart into Mary and all of the participants. There was no way I could have stayed in a professional objective position where Mary was concerned. I was grieving and growing weary. I wasn't sure I could keep going.

I didn't even have time to take in a restful breath before the next discouraging words came to stifle my troubled spirit: The Day Care Center was going to fold in only 90 days. The government didn't find

A Plan For You

the program necessary any longer; they needed the money for something else - maybe their pockets. My boss suggested that I be laid off so I could rest and prepare for finding another job. We'd all be looking for work soon.

I went on unemployment and researched other job possibilities. I didn't have it in me to be a care giver any longer. "God, anything else - something fun, like an aerobics instructor," I prayed. So I went out and applied at a few places and was in total unbelief when I found what they paid. I was good enough for the job, but the pay wasn't good enough for me.

Being on unemployment was awful: I had to give up dance lessons, Jim had to give up karate lessons right before he was to become a brown belt. We had absolutely no spending money. I couldn't make my car payments, so I borrowed money from Daddy Frank to pay off my car so I could have transportation. I started using my charge card to buy food. The financial struggle added to my already depressed state. I needed to get a job and quickly.

Searching the newspaper, I found an Activity Director position over in my friend Brandy's neck of the woods, but the pay couldn't keep a boat a float, therefore I was about to sink.

So add the commute, with remaining as a care giver, only now in skilled nursing, plus making as much money as I had made on unemployment, and this equals: depression mixed with insanity.

After having a successful job with good pay, and providing fun activities for my son and me, I began to hate myself for not being able to do better for us.

A Plan For You

I blamed all of the misfortune on to myself. God certainly wasn't helping me. Satan was messing with my mind, convincing me that I was rejected by God, and that I deserved to be punished.

One day I looked at my weary reflection in the mirror. The person looking back at me was a pathetic loser, getting nowhere in life. I couldn't provide for my son or myself. Yet, I kept going to work and giving to the job as best I could, doing the drive, making peanut pay and hardly able to afford peanut butter.

"God hates you! You're a worthless piece of crap!" I shouted at the reflection.

But yelling wasn't enough, so I began punching myself in the face over and over, yelling, "I hate you! Even God hates you!" Then I started crying louder than I ever remember. The agony was like none I had never known. I thought about how God had taken Marcie from me and now He'd stripped me of my finances and the little life pleasures Jim and I once enjoyed. Separation from God is the worst feeling; it is literally Hell.

I related to Mary so much at that moment. If Satan can get a person to belief they are worthless they can't hear the voice of Jesus calling to them. And I was there and didn't know how to take in my next breath, as life was killing me. "Jesus, please love me and help me!" I moaned out loud.

Blessings Flow

Chapter 10

JoDee and Brandy were comforting friends. They truly understood me when I told them of my mirror terror. JoDee and Brandy believed in Jesus and were open to talking about Him with me. None of us were exactly living for Him, but we believed strongly in Him.

They didn't think I was crazy. They had open ears and big hearts for me. I was and would be a comfort to these friends as well.

Brandy would understand because she had suffered a nervous breakdown where she experienced spiritual and hell like visions, just before we became friends.

JoDee would later suffer from a level of darkness that would become an out of body terror for her.

JoDee lived next door to me and I worked very close to Brandy. So my comforting friends were right there when I needed them or vise versa.

But other important people were placed in my life. Bill helped me out with food and was great company.

A Plan For You

He didn't know of my mirror terror and neither did my son. But my son knew I was troubled by my depressed behavior, yet again, and he was a wise child and was able to read between mama's dark spells.

Jim's coach heard of our troubles when there was the possibility we would have to move closer to my job and he'd have to give up wrestling. Coach Mike took a special liking to Jim. He did favor him and saw potential for a star wrestler. No matter the struggle, I couldn't take him away from a school where someone cared and believed in him and that he enjoyed attending. He'd already given up karate, due to lack of money.

He was graceful in making it look like he didn't want the lessons any longer, and told me he wanted to focus on wrestling. He liked the competition and challenge of wrestling.

Coach came over one evening baring gifts of food and a collection of money. He hoped we could stay, but understood if we'd have to move. His healthy interest in Jim and my well-being seemed to echo an answer from the Lord: We were to remain in our present living situation. And Jim had a friend in this man, who would be a strong example of a God loving just like his Grandpa Frank.

Then another blessing came in a strange, but miraculous way. Nine years after Ben and I divorced, I received child support. With this money we were able to live more comfortably. Jim's high school years were good years, memorable years thanks to Coach Mike and neighbor Bill who cared about his success. **And** assuredly, so did God!

My Men

Chapter 11

When Jim finished high school we moved closer to work, as he was going to take up wrestling in the college located in that neighborhood, as suggested by Coach Mike. He took on a job at McDonalds and attended the college for one quarter and decided that it wasn't for him, and then took a job with my old flame and friend, Will, setting up mobile homes.

Will had remained a part of our lives through the 10 years that we had been separated, even during his marriage with Brandy. We rekindled our friendship when we saw one another at a mutual friend's wedding. We attempted to rekindle our romance, but it just wasn't happening. We would remain closely connected friends and this would baffle our family and friends, as they believed we should be more.

Jim decided he would make more money working for Will than at McDonald's, so he was glad to take on the position.

A Plan For You

I recall a time when Jim and I were riding our bikes together, just a few years before he had graduated from high school. We noticed some men working on a roof. Jim said, "That's the kind of job I'm gonna' have, I ain't gonna' work in no boring office." Being the hyper young man that he was, I believed that comment to be true.

So after a muddy, messy season of setting up mobile homes, Jim made the decision to attend a technical college, where he got a good paying job for an airfreight company working in an office. So this is a lesson on that old cliché, "Never say Never."

He gladly earned his keep by paying rent. He learned that my inability to give him everything that he wanted was a positive occurrence, as when he bought his own car and clothes and paid his own way in life, he appreciated and took care of the things that he purchased. He also learned that he wasn't going to be poor as an adult, and was willing to do what he needed to avoid financial struggle. And helping me gave him a good feeling. He was now the grown man of the house.

Will was a friend to me and Brandy, and was good to our children. He provided jobs for them and demonstrated other supporting ways to help them. He was a good man with a good heart.

I was content with our friendship. I liked not having to be intimate. If only I could have had this mind-set years earlier; it may have saved me a lot of heart ache.

Will and I had grown in the Lord through our years of separation. Having God in common enriched our friendship, and was about to become even stronger in Him through another hell spell, I was headed for.

When Will I Smile Again

My Father,
When will I smile again?
I am with much weariness
I have lost my dreams
Where are you?
I need you so.
When will my heart smile again?
I am a young woman.
My spirit is growing old.
Where are you?
I need you so.
When will my heart smile again?
I am with much fear
This feeling is uncomfortable.
Where are you?
I need you.
When will my heart smile again?
Heal my darkened spirit
Free me from this despair.
I need you so.

Cross to Bear

Chapter 12

Work was reaching a stressful level, in that, I was burning out and felt I was going to work in a nursing home until I became a patient in one. I was also dealing with a "nose to the grind stone, no non-sense boss," which wasn't intentionally or knowingly hurting me, but she had a low tolerance for weakness, and the deeper I went into depression, the harder it was for me to hide my affliction from her, or anyone.

My boss was academically intelligent; I admired her for her smarts. I worked along side of her for 5 years. I was able to overlook her firm ways for most of those years. I know that she appreciated me and that's what kept me going to work.

However, in my weakness, which was now reaching a crippling level, I felt her strict characteristic rise over me, and I was uncomfortable around her. I could tell that she wasn't pleased with me. Perhaps this was her psychological challenge.

A Plan For You

I hated myself when I was down and was hard enough on myself without the reminders from someone else that I was useless in my weakness.

By now, I was discovering that this affliction was my life challenge to battle, (my cross to bear). Most often it was brought on circumstantially and psychologically. There was always a reason behind it. I don't believe it stemmed from a chemical imbalance in my brain. It was an imbalance in my brain, all right – but let us take a look into the window of pain and sorrow I had already lived through from the beginning of my life.

Spirit Lifters

I always made a few close friends wherever I worked. God had placed people in my life that cared about me – flaws and all. I needed to be around people that would lift my spirits when I was down. And not wanting anyone to feel as depressed as I could get, I learned to be a spirit lifter with true compassion. A gift from God was transpiring; my words would become my strength in my weakness and be an inspiration to others.

Gertrude and Cindy were the ones who helped me through this intense time at this work place.

Gertrude was my German friend and she seemed to see strength in me that I couldn't see. She was strong, tall and beautiful, but under her strong exterior lingered a soft spirit. She was fun to be around and her backward American sayings made me laugh. But Gertrude was proud to be an American.

I'll never forget the time she went into the staff lounge where several employees were speaking their native language, and she sharply commanded in her German accent: "You live in America, speak English!"

And I saw inside her heart when we went to see the Movie *Shindler's List* together. Of all movies for my German friend, who had lived through some of that war time experience as a girl, to watch? She broke down in tears and said, "I hate Germans." Gertrude didn't really mean that. I believe, not only was she proud to be an American; she also appreciated being German. But the movie was heart wrenching. And I loved Gertrude's heart.

Cindy reminded me of my sister, Stormy, in many ways. But she had a gift that was all her own; she may not have been aware of it, but I appreciated her words of encouragement. She was easy going and easy to talk to. She was honest and straight forward; she was real. Cindy didn't like people she cared about to feel bad or sad, so she encouraged them. She had a special way of leaving a person's ego attached. And with my struggle with depression, she was just the right friend to have around.

I related to her and her husband, Ralph. They rode a Harley-Davidson, and knew biker people. Her husband was everybody's buddy; meaning that he was generous and kind by nature. Cindy and He were childhood sweet hearts, and a couple that I felt comfortable and enjoyed being around.

Cindy and Stormy were similar in appearance; they loved riding behind their man on motorcycles;

and were fun loving in character and enjoyed partying with friends, their husbands were well-liked. Cindy did not have Stormy's mean streak. I'm not saying she didn't have a temper; it just was not as noticeable as Stormy's was.

And Stormy and Cindy would share a similar tragic experience.

(See later chapter).

Paper Turns to Rock

Chapter 13

I tossed and turned, kicking the covers off the side of my bed. I heard someone at the door. My sleep had been so heavy, since I was struggling with a deep depression. Waking up was a challenge. I heard a louder noise at the door. The intruder was shoving it open.

My first response was to check on Jim, because I felt the intruder was going to kill him first, then rape and kill me. But I wasn't going to let him touch my son; although Jim was a strong young man and could have handled the intruder. But I wasn't going to let this stranger get near him, and I didn't feel there was enough time to prevent the potential murders that the intruder was intending.

I met him in the hall way. He was wearing all tan clothing. He had stringy long blond hair and an evil smile. I didn't have time to notice his eyes.

I immediately started beating him with my hands, choking and kicking him. I felt so heavy and tired,

A Plan For You

but knew I must kill him. He fought me into Jim's room where he was still asleep and undisturbed by what was happening.

Now, he was too close to my son and my strength increased enough to kill the man and he fell dead to the floor.

I stared at his body and I watched him turn to a piece of paper with a rock on top.

Yes, it was a dream. The intruder of all my nightmares has been Satan. He was constantly after my spirit. The closer I'd get to Jesus, the more nightmares I endured.

But this particular dream had a message about my writing. Unbeknownst to me, my writing was going to become my strength. The paper was representing my writing and the rock represented Jesus covering my writing.

Broken Heart Assurance

Without sensitivity, tears and pain,
there can be no gain.
I know that it feels as though the end is near,
when your heart is filled with so much
anguish and fear.
When your heart is broken and
filled with despair,
you try to depart from the pain by telling
yourself you just don't care.
You want to run so desperately, but you
don't know where.
It just seems as though life isn't very fair.
You must grasp God's hand.
He will certainly understand.
Be assured he will comfort you
through and through,
He never leaves you during these sad times;
this is so very true.
I know you find it hard to believe that your
heart is filled with love;
and that our Father is gently smiling at you
from above.
Be glad for your sensitivity, tears and pain;
For your endurance of them will enrich
you with much gain.

A Promise

Chapter 14

In my hopeless state, I continued to write rhyming poetry. It never dawned on me that there were other ways to write them. And every time I got low in spirit, I'd write poems and read the Bible in parts (it may interest people to know that I was not a reader and that it still takes me a very long time to read a book, which adds more interest to this story).

JoDee and I were destined to be neighbors, as each time I moved there she was - nearly next door. We started studying the Bible, as we were both searching for answers from God, and needed our spirits lifted. But instead of lifting us up, we became more confused. (Of course it did not help to study Revelation while in a down state-of –mind.)

The more we got into the Bible, the more visits from the power of darkness we experienced. JoDee had her out of body experience, where she saw herself stab herself, and my nightmares increased.

Satan would come disguised as someone I love or famous people:

Come With Me

I stood on the beach in my pink sweats, no makeup and messy hair, looking like I just got out of bed. I felt comfortable with my appearance; even though bathing beauties in their bikinis lay all over the beach.

A handsome young man, looking like Fabio, approached me, "I love you and want you to come with me."

I looked at my surroundings, all of the gorgeous gals with perfect bodies, and asked, "Why would you be interested in me when you got all these beautiful women to choose from?"

"It is you I want; you are more special than them."

I looked into his eyes and realized who he was. He already had the girls on the beach.

"Satan, I belong to Jesus. I don't know why you bother me so much. You need to turn your life over to Jesus. You know that's the only way."

He looked at me; his expression turned sad and hopeless as he knew that he would not ever accept Jesus, and he knew he didn't have me this time. He has a mission and it is to destroy the name of Jesus.

I was in search of my mission. I had lost all motivation and had no dreams and desires. I needed more for my life; more than being an accomplished dancer, an exercise nut, a sky diver, an Activity

Director. Being an overachiever comes with a lot of let downs; especially when there is a lot of self-serving in them. My mission light had not clicked on, even though God was shining the answer right in my face.

My son was concerned when he saw me stay home more, turn down offers to go and do things with friends, and changed my appearance.

He looked at me one day and said, "What is wrong with you; your hair looks like an old lady and you're dressin' and actin' like one. You don't do anything anymore."

Even my friend Brandy thought so. True friends are upfront with you. She took a before and after picture, which she would show me later.

It was true; I was becoming a hopeless old lady.

I continued to write poems to God and spent desperate times praying to Him for help to bring more purpose to my life. I wanted the missing ingredient.

By no coincidence I was compelled to get an electric typewriter, as I had handwritten my many poems and thought I should type them and make them into a booklet.

I discovered that I remembered how to type from my high school days. So I typed the pages up, added Marcie's poems; then took the manuscript (if you will) to a printer to copy the pages, staple them together, and put on a cover to form my first book ever: *Out of My Heart*. It may not be anything to write home about, but it gave me a lot of comfort and satisfaction, and most of all, it was moving me toward my mission in life.

A Plan For You

Shortly after I wrote the book of rhyming poetry, I lie in bed and strongly felt the presence of Jesus. The light was becoming transparent. And out of my mouth came these words: "Lord, I wanna' go to college and learn to write, and if you will get me through school, I promise, I will write for you."

No, and I did not live happily ever after. Giving back my gift to Jesus would entail unbelievable hard work and conviction; and, oh yeah, spiritual warfare. Satan was not pleased at all with my promise.

Surprising Support

Chapter 15

Unbelievable things started happening, as I was in the beginning stages of finding my mission. I wanted to share my *Out of Heart* booklet with family and friends, especially if there was a poem about that particular person or persons.

While writing it, I thought of people who had made an impact on my life and had more to do with my faith in Jesus than they realized. So I wrote a letter and added it to the book; even though I felt as though I would never see or hear from them.

Reverend Teshera, *12-7-89*

There is so much I wish to say to you. You made quite an impact on my life. I don't believe you ever knew how much.

Even though I haven't seen you in 26 years, I often think of you.

A Plan For You

It was you and your wife that taught me about Jesus, and I thank you.

When you left the church I was deeply saddened, I missed you so much. You were like a father to me at that time in my life.

Now I realize, you taught me what the Lord desired me to know. It was just enough and then it was time for you to move on with your teachings. Isn't it wonderful to know God is perfect in his planning. We are to be more like Jesus in all we do and you displayed that so well. You displayed this so beautifully. Jesus definitely lives in your heart.

I remember all of the fun activities you put on for the children of the church. You were good to us. I remember singing in the choir. I remember how special my Baptism was to me; but most important of all, was my acceptance of Jesus. I was only 11 years old. This is still the most important event to ever occur in my life.

I left the church shortly after you did. I strayed from God as well. Even though I did stray, your teachings lingered in my heart. God has His way of calling us back home to Him. Amen

I just wanted to take the time to thank you, and to tell you that I love you.

As I reread this letter I realize I needed some education, but the content is amazing and it fits well with where my testimony has been (as read in *Time to Come Home)* and where it is heading in this book.

I thought to myself, wouldn't it be nice if I could locate the Tesheras and give them a book so they

A Plan For You

could read this letter and see the poems I had written for God.

I couldn't release this thought and decided to try and contact the old church on the campgrounds where all the members had transferred, and where I had last attended prior to leaving the church. Although it had been 26 years since I'd seen them, maybe there would be someone left at that old church that might know the location of the Tesheras.

And with one call, I located there whereabouts and would I ever be surprised: They were living in Lynnwood, Washington where they were pasturing a church, about an hours drive away.

I mailed them a book and they were surprised to hear from me. We had a reunion and stayed in touch through letters. They would become one of my biggest supporters of my goal to write for God.

Pastor James remained a faithful supporter as well. We kept in contact through letter writing, as he had moved to Colorado a short time following Marcie's death.

God has placed surprising supporters in my life!

Mission Moving

Chapter 16

I called Brandy who was now living in Alaska. (Some friends remained close no matter the miles that separated us). I shared with her that I was going to college to learn to write, and that I was going to write a best seller for Jesus. In saying that, I was inspired and felt confident about what I was going to accomplish. There was no doubt in my voice.

Brandy had seen me accomplish many goals and do daring things through our 13 year friendship. She responded, "You scare me when you do that!" Brandy believed every word.

I moved onward into the mission and school was a challenge. But I was determined and would do whatever it took to make this dream and my promise to Jesus come true.

I worked harder than many, as I had learning blockers - probably stemming from old messages and memories of being called dumb blank, while at the same time having my head slapped to remind me, even more intensely, of my stupidity. And then there's the fact that I'd rather be a character in a book than studying or reading one.

I met some inspiring teachers who helped me and seemed to see my dedication and drive to succeed, and not just by passing a class, but getting the most out of it to learn how to be a good writer, and by taking on some of the most challenging news story assignments.

Susan was my journalism instructor and she was fun and serious; she taught me much about writing. She gave no easy way out; I worked to learn.

I recall a time when I was writing a news story on the computer and I couldn't figure out how to spell a word (one of those words you needed to know how to spell in order to find it in the dictionary). I asked other students in the room how to spell it, and Susan stopped others from rescuing me, "Look it up in the dictionary!"

I searched for about 30 minutes before finding the word in the dictionary. She was always telling the students to look it up in the dictionary or the Stylebook.

I had encouraging friends helping me through the classes that we attended together: Markie and Lynda.

Markie was super intelligent and learning seemed to come easy for her, she was a helpful friend to have around. We were both 40 years old. And to start college at this age meant we were serious about being there. She always asked me questions about myself. At first I was a little taken back by the questions, but learned she was truly interested in me as an individual, and it was easy sharing with her. For some reason my life fascinated her.

Lynda was young enough to be my daughter. She served in the military and was going to college to earn a Master's in Communication. She was beautiful, natural curly brown hair and big brown eyes. She looked like a model or movie star; she looked similar to Julia Roberts. But she wasn't in the least bit interested in being a model or acting like one. She was in school with a goal in mind.

I had a goal to learn all that I could about writing. Not to become a newspaper writer when I graduated, but a book writer for Jesus. However, I had the essential drive to become a good reporter and columnist for a newspaper. My two new friends would help me through my most challenging assignments. Being editors, reporters and columnists for the college newspaper was exciting. We helped each other through the ups and downs of life and school.

Being that I had thrill seeking and goal getting in my system, it only seemed natural to take on difficult assignments. I drove all the way to Wenatchee and back in a day to meet and write a story on Mayor Norm Rice, who had been an alumnus at the college, as well as an editor for the paper. The next story assignment that I chose caused Satan to haunt the hell out of me.

A Plan For You

Drive Inn Devils

I was standing at a drive inn theatre. Young men and women in black leather jackets surrounded me. Evil was evident, as I saw it in their faces. I began to tremble in fear. I looked on the movie screen to see them devouring a human being, eating flesh and blood. They were doing this insane act at the very place I stood in the lot, and they wanted me to see what they were intending to do to me. The evil overwhelmed me to the point of making my tongue as thick as their darkness. I was standing among demons and devil worshippers. My mind was thinking the word, "Jesus." I struggled to call His name. After several silent attempts, His name became clear on my lips and I awoke.

And did this dream stop me from completing the story on Satanism that I had vastly been researching – of course not. My interest in this assignment stemmed from a pastor coming to the college to tell us about the neighborhood groups of practicing Satanists and because of my strong faith in Jesus, after all He was the reason I was going to college.

My research on this story started to mentally drench my mind; the nightmares continued. I was trying my best to be objective as a reporter, but I knew too much about Jesus. I contacted religious groups that were considered occults, as stated by the visiting Pastor and other spiritual leaders. I researched the Bible; I discovered that a few groups would not acknowledge Jesus as God; I went to a concert of a former High Priest of Satan who revealed many

A Plan For You

gruesome secrets about the sick practices of Lucifer's followers.

I felt I was well informed and had gathered enough data to write the story, but to do so objectively, and to put it to words - this would be more than a challenge.

Susan, Markie and Lynda noticed my strange behavior and were concerned. My two friends asked me to consider not doing the story, especially when Lynda and I were working on our assignments alone one evening and I had discovered the Church of Satan's phone number. I had every intention of calling the number but Lynda stopped me, and most assuredly, God stopped me Himself.

Susan requested that I see the school psychologist. I was open with the counselor of my belief and why this was hard to write objectively. I mentioned the gruesome nightmares I was enduring. My mind was freaked out, but I wanted to complete the assignment. The counselor was a Christian so he understood what I was battling. After a few sessions with him, I followed through and completed the story. I ran into problems getting it in print, as I lost it on the computer and had to rewrite it. But mine and God's mission were accomplished.

Here's My Father

*Let me introduce you to my
Father;
the Man of glory, the Man
of grace
He sent Jesus to save me;
the Son of God, the Lord of
peace
He's the sparkle in my eyes
and the joy in my smile
He's the warmth of my soul
and the ruler of my heart
So let me introduce you to
my Father;
the Lord of love, the Lord
of life
He sent Jesus to save me;
a precious gift, a gift I
praise
He's the rock that I stand on
and the mountain that I
climb
He's the shine on my face
and the flow from my mouth
So let me introduce you to
my Father;
the God of wonder, the God
of joy
He sent Jesus to save us;
to lift us up, to bring us
home!*

Fixed on Jesus

*He is not visible
yet His face is
most beautiful, most
glorious
of all
I know as I see Him in my
heart -
He is not touchable
yet His touch is
most gentle, most loving
of all
I know as he touches my
heart -
He does not speak in my
ear
yet His voice is
most audible, most heard
of all
I know as he speaks to my
heart -
Through faith I will
see His glorious face
touch His gentle hands
hear His precious voice
in heaven
forever!*

Why do You Bother

I woke up in my bedroom. I was wearing some flowered pajamas, the ones I had on before going to bed that night. My room looked the same as usual. Was I dreaming?

Jim stood over me. He stared into my eyes. These were not my son's eyes. I then realized who my intruder was. I was terrified of His presence. My heart felt like it stopped, as I fell into darkness. I called out to Jesus, then opened my eyes to see Satan still standing over me. I mustered up enough strength to produce a strong statement, "I know it's you Satan. Why do you bother me; you know I belong to Jesus."

Off to Church We Go

Chapter 17

Will and I remained friends, and he was concerned about my encounters and spiritual struggles. I shared my nightmares with him and being a believer, he was ready to help me.

He suggested we start going to church – a small Bible teaching church less than a mile from his place. Being in college, I also needed some financial help, so I worked cleaning his company shop. Just one of the jobs I had during college. I also cleaned apartments where I lived, and worked as an editor for the newspaper in college. My plate was full and my pursuit was troubling, trying and down right tiring. But I did what I had to do to complete my promise to Jesus.

At the request of Will, I saw the Pastor, and shared the details of what I was enduring. He called it what it truly was: "Spiritual Warfare." Those who are close to Jesus will battle Satan and his demons. A

A Plan For You

person might want to say halleluiah about now, but this wasn't very fun.

Church was good for my spirit. I became involved and was able to share my written talents, which had much improved from the education I was obtaining. I wrote this book's theme poem, *A Plan For You*, and the aforementioned poems, as well as others, for special events in the church. I felt my writing was pleasing to the congregation and especially God.

My writing and life had more meaning through attending church. I was stronger in faith and obtaining Bible knowledge. The more my faith strengthened the more spiritual warfare I'd endure. Satan would not stop me from my dream. My determination would earn me rewards and favor from God that would push Satan back in his pit, but only long enough for him to come up with other strategies in attempt to shake my faith.

Best Blessings

Chapter 18

My most treasured blessings in life are my children, my family and my friends. It seems that the friends that God placed in my life were for His purpose and on purpose. They were my best blessings. Human life has more value than material wealth.

Mindy was working for Will as the company secretary. She was also Will's roommate - Percy's, girlfriend.

Mindy and I were so similar in appearance that we could have been sisters. Not only were we similar in looks, but we were the same age with sons close in age. Our friendship came on quickly, as though we had known each other all of our lives. Just the way my other close friends and I meshed instantaneously.

Mindy was more mellow than my other close friends. She was similar to Brandy in that she liked to go out and see the world; but Mindy planned out details before going out, and then carefully explored

A Plan For You

---

the globe, and Brandy said, "Let's go" and we were gone getting a quick look at this place called earth.

When shopping with Mindy, it was important to plan the day, as she would not miss a thing in the store. Items would be closely observed. I have never known a shopper like Mindy. Everything was cute, or so and so would like this, or this would look good somewhere. She was always thinking of others when shopping. I was one of those whom she often bought for. If she bought something for herself; I needed one too. I appreciated her thoughtfulness and her *stop and smell the rose's* character.

She handled my ups and downs and the dark spell I was encountering. A true friend does not leave a friend in darkness, but attempts to lighten the way for them. Most people would hear what I was going through and say, "Stay away from that woman, she's a nut case."

I did not push Jesus down anyone's throat; it's not His style. He prefers people come to love Him on their own free will. But my faith in Jesus was at a higher level and more prominent and forthright. Therefore my friends knew where I stood with Jesus. I had my joy, even in the midst of the spiritual warfare. My true friends saw that joy and witnessed that special strength in me and stayed with me during my darkest hours, they were my best blessings.

Education is more than worth the struggle
(Written as an Opinion for college paper
May 18, 1990)

Many students struggle to keep going. The pressure of juggling school, homework, jobs, families, friends and the necessary business of life can be more than one person can bear.

I know it's difficult. As a student, single mother and employee, I have to juggle a number of obligations; but in the fall of 1989 I returned to college because I suffered job burnout. In spite of the chaos, I don't regret what I've done because I am an advocate of education for a special reason.

My daughter Marcie died May 22, 1979 of liver cancer at age nine.

Education took priority with Marcie. Her interest in school began when she was 4 years old. She manipulated her way into school.

Her brother Jim was 5 years old and it was his first day of school. Marcie decided it would be her first day as well. With the school located across the street from our apartment, this would be easy. She waited until I was in the shower, then she quickly put on her dress she had previously chosen for this special occasion. She made it to the school in the nick of time because the kindergarteners had gone into the class room. Marcie walked up to the teacher and said, "I'm sorry I'm late, but my mother was sewing my dress." The teacher welcomed her into the class room.

A Plan For You

At 7 years old, Marcie and her girl friend had a discussion about their futures. Her girlfriend planned to get married at 17 and have 10 children. Marcie planned to go to college, get married at 25 and have 2 children.

When she was 8, I attended a school conference with her teachers to discuss the fact that she was doing junior high school work.

At 9 years old, during her illness, she asked me if she could live with me until she was 23, because she would graduate from college by then.

When I graduate and get my degree, I'll hold it in the air and say, "This one's for you Marcie."

In spite of all the chaos, I'm not going to give up, because I have something to go for. Life's too short.

A Miracle in May

Chapter 19

May 22, 1991, exactly 12 years after Marcie's death, it was award's night at the college. My instructor Susan informed me that I must be there.

An assembly of students filled the room, many to be honored for their extra efforts and excellent grades. I went way above the ordinary and worked harder than the majority of students to make good grades. Although I lived with the dumb blank syndrome, part of that crippling message was true; I was a slow learner. Then add the fact Satan was attempting to kill my dream, and my odds of being successful wouldn't be a trip down happy trails; it would be more like skidding on my knees on a concrete road, bleeding and none-the-less keep pressing toward the happy trails. Talk about the school of hard knocks; that was a literal cliché statement when it related to me and school. But my gift of determination and faith in God would progress me through these great odds.

A Plan For You

I earned a 3.5 grade level, and made the Dean's list every quarter, surprising myself. But still it wasn't the highest level to earn, and I knew Marki had reached that top elevation; she aced her classes, and her stories were well written and done so without a lot of mistakes or rewrites. Sure she was challenged, but I was way more challenged. Oh to have been blessed with a quick learning brain. I spent much time and many hours on all stories and other assignments that were related to my curriculum.

I went to school in the summer so I could get through school more quickly, or for the mere fact, to stay caught up with my intelligent friends so we could graduate together.

One hot summer day, I was working on an assignment for an art class, I spent most of my summer days working on the classes that I took and made no time for fun. Jim noticed how hard I was working and insisted I make a picnic lunch and that we go to the beach. "Come on, Mom, it'll be good for you to get away from your school work for awhile." And he was right; it felt good to take a break. We hadn't done this since he was a 14, entering high school, and didn't want to hang out with mom anymore. It was a special day that brought back good memories. But I didn't take many more breaks that summer.

As I watched people get their awards, I thought I might get an award for my stories on Satanism and Mayor Norm Rice; I had received certificates for them.

Susan stood before the podium, as I sat in curiosity as to why I was there. A few students were

A Plan For You

called forward: Marki, Lynda and I were among them. We were given an achievement award for our contributions to the college paper. I thought, okay, this is the award that I'm here for. I was presented a beautiful plaque. I was pleased; no I was shocked by any of my accomplishments in school.

Marki was called up again; I knew she was earning the highest achievement award and I was glad for her. Then my name was called. I was puzzled as I listened to Susan make a positive speech about Marki and awarded her the top award in journalism. Then she made one about me; I could hardly believe it. I wish I could have taped what she said as I was so excited and I don't recall much of what she said. But her speech brought tears to my eyes. She presented me with my plaque, the Scholastic Achievement Award in Journalism.

In all my excitement, my hair stood on end, as I recognized the presence of Jesus. His heavenly presence shined the spotlight on me. I knew He and Marcie were with me at that moment. My already teary eyes filled up and came past the surface trickling down my cheeks. I felt an internal joy as I held my award the air and said, "This one's for you Marcie." I felt as though there was a big celebration in my honor in heaven on that day.

Busted, Broke and Bruised

Chapter 20

Graduation night was another highlight in my life. I managed to graduate with Marki and Lynda. My folks and Will came for this major event. Being at the center of attention and recognizing I was in the presence and favor of Jesus brought inexpressible excitement and joy. I was ready to take on the world. I would go out and write my best seller without any problem, the worst was over.

After college there was the job of looking for a job. I had to make a living while I wrote my book. I didn't have the college paper position any longer. I wasn't cleaning apartments, as Jim and I had sense then found a small house to rent.

So while I searched for a decent paying position; I continued to clean Will's company shop; I worked for an older friend cleaning her house and keeping her yard groomed and pruned; then I spent a day with JoDee, and her soon to be husband, in the business of selling coupons to people and businesses in the community. I made $5.00, as the deal was you got money if people bought the coupon book. Needless-to-say, I was not good at selling to people over the phone. And I wasn't very good at accepting sales calls over my own phone, but desperate measures.

I managed to earn enough to keep the rent paid and food in our mouths. It was helpful to have a son who was willfully earning his keep by paying a portion of the rent.

Finally, Coach Mike, whom Jim was still in contact with and visiting, told me about a job in a department store in our neighborhood. His friend was supervisor of the clothing section. He was certain I would make at least $8.00 an hour and benefits were good. I applied and got the job. I made $5.25 and was only able to work part time; therefore benefits weren't accessible to me, and I paid union dues. But I was grateful to have a steady job, even though I made the same amount working at the college. I was able to get by, but there was no spending or fun money.

I had to give up my job at Will's shop, but stayed in close contact with him, as we were still attending church together. And I spent time with his secretary Mindy, as our friendship was quickly growing.

When in retail the hours can be unpredictable. I remember once working nine days in a row before getting a day off. I did what I had to do to survive.

After six months of retail work, Brandy invited me to come to Alaska and work the summer. She was sure I'd make good money and could put some away.

A Plan For You

Jim was a responsible young man of 22 years. He could manage the house for the summer, and I'd send money for rent, as I'd be making a bunch.

One of my jobs in Alaska was working for the semi-pro ball team, the Pilots. I worked with Brandy in the souvenir booth and I sold 50/50 tickets to people in the stands. My time in Alaska was cut short when I was clobbered, no literally knocked out, by a baseball speeding at my forehead at 90 miles per hour. I got two black eyes and an autograph from player that knocked me out. I realized what a true friend Brandy was when she wiped the vomit from my face. We both laughed when I said, "Is that tootsie rolls?" I had been eating them at the park that day. My head ached, but we had a good laugh!

I returned home with the shiners, and a lot of dizziness, but I had to immediately go looking for work. I had to explain to people that I wasn't a victim of abuse, and not so sure they all believed me.

JoDee and her now husband, Kevin were living a few blocks away. Again, we were in the same neighborhood. They were working for a plastic company and the owner was looking for a receptionist. I applied and got the job. I learned quickly and did a good work. But I watched the boss literally yell and call people stupid and dummy, or I'd call up to his office and hear him downgrading the girls upstairs. I lasted about seven months there – that was too long. I lived through enough name calling in my life to put up with a verbally abusive boss.

Then I watched Brandy's daughter, Kitty's two children, cleaned houses and went back to cleaning

A Plan For You

Will's shop and I made a little over $500.00 a month. The struggle hit me hard, and I went into a depression that I just lived with like it was no big deal.

I went to the clinic for a regular womanly check up and the Nurse Practitioner asked me how I was doing, and I responded, "I've been depressed." I nonchalantly responded. But it was a big deal to her, and she wanted me to see the social worker.

It was normal to lie in bed and wish I wouldn't wake up, or to have my mind so messed up I would think of ways to take myself out that wouldn't appear to look like suicide. Not that I would really commit such an act as Jim came to my forefront and we did need one another. But I did let the crazy thoughts run through my mind. It was normal to drag myself through a day without an ounce of energy for life. It was normal to have nightmares with Satan taunting me. A person that experienced depression as much as I had would simply find familiarity with the illness.

This season was a killer season: take the tragedy of Cindy's husband, Ralph dying of cancer, then add a death of a friend and coworker, Mary from my past nursing home job dying of a heart attack, as well as, Brandy having an aneurism and nearly dying, and Marty having one just a few months before, then add the fact that they were all close to my age, and I'm in a crisis situation. Where are you God?

Heard

Am I heard
My desperation – My devastation
Am I heard
My struggling – My suffering
Am I heard
My worrying – My wondering
Am I hearing you
Your promises – Your plans
or am I
merely missing the answers?

Let Me

Let me love my weak self too –
Let me see the strength
in being fragile –
Let me not fight
to make my
sensitive self
go away –
Let me love every part of my being -
Let me grow to understand
that you love
all that I am

Attending to Others

Chapter 21

My German friend, Gertrude kept me updated on Cindy's condition following Ralph's death. Her drinking went out of control and she didn't care about living without Ralph. (My sister, Stormy would deal with the same devasating situation years later). As I had mentioned their life styles and appearances were similar. My heart hurt for my young friend, and I didn't know what it felt like to lose the love of your life, but I did know what it felt like to lose a child – and death hurts! And then later Gertrude informed of our mutual friend and coworker, Mary's death. I wasn't able to do much except to pray for Cindy and Mary's family. The affect that these deaths and tragedies had on me was like being stranded in the middle of the ocean on a raft and not caring if a rescue takes place.

But God!

I spent hours in prayer and wrote spiritual poems, and I kept sharing them with the church. I wasn't able

A Plan For You

to tithe much, but I shared my writing and cleaned the church and did volunteer work to help others, even less fortunate than me.

Getting away from self was apparently what God had in mind, as Brandy was flown back to Seattle to get help from specialists and necessary therapy. She would be where her mother and children were closely located, and I would play a part in her recovery.

I visited Brandy in the hospital a few days a week. She had lost her memory. But thank God, she knew me.

She wandered through the hospital one day looking for a store to buy a comb, and she didn't have any hair, as it was shaved off from her surgeries. After that a wander guard was placed on her, but it wasn't affective as Brandy knew the code to get out.

When she was released from the hospital to her mom's place, I came to walk with her and encourage her to exercise and tried to keep her memory fresh. I brought photos to share of when she and the kids were young and I think she thought we were younger.

Brandy recovered a lot slower than Marty did from her aneurism, but then Brandy was affected on both sides of the brain. And it had a major affect on her overall health.

I spent hours in prayer for Brandy's recovery and after a few months her memory was more clear and she returned home to Alaska with her husband. Over time her memory improved, as did her physical strength. She still walks with special shoes and moves slowly. But she is walking and she resumed working.

I don't know if my caring for Brandy was a fair exchange for her attending to me when I was laid out with a concussion from a flying baseball, and she tended to me, even wiping vomit from my face. But her life being spared was a miracle and I thank God.

Thank You

Did I remember to thank you
while in my tales of woe
to have faith in you
while in a fit of anger
to trust your written promises
while weeping hopelessly
to lean on your undying love
while in deep despair
Did I remember to tell you
that I am sorry
for forgetting?

Filled To the Brim

Chapter 22

My little house was filled to the brim with family and friends the Christmas of 1994. My parents, my sisters and their husbands and one niece, Percy and Mindy, Marty and her new husband, Tony, and of course Will came. Jim and I had spent so many years going to California to spend time with my family, that they felt it was time they all came to us, and they wanted to cheer me up after going through such a rough time with depression and sick and dying friends.

I knew they were coming and I had no money for gifts, so I spent hours with my crafted friend JoDee and made personalized gifts for all of them. I wrote a poem about each family member and put them in a cloth frame.

Being poor had its rewards; I recall a few Christmases where JoDee and I were low on money. I had borrowed her sewing machine when I was making costumes for dancing, and she needed to buy

A Plan For You

gifts for her two girls. I took her shopping on my credit card in trade for the sewing machine. JoDee said it was one of her best Christmases.

Another Christmas, she didn't have money for a Christmas tree. So we decided to go out into the woods and cut one down illegally – what's a friend for? I wanted her to have a tree. We couldn't find a good one so we started to drive back to her home when we saw a tree lot that had trees for sale for six dollars. I had exactly six dollars and I was glad to buy my friend a Christmas tree. But the story of giving doesn't end here...

When we returned to JoDee's home, as she pulled out her decorations her daughters told her about a neighboring family that had nothing up for Christmas; they were poor and didn't have much to eat. So JoDee went through her decorations, boxed some up along with some cookies, candy and food items and later that evening, she and her daughters placed the gift box on neighbor's front porch.

As I review this story, I see God's love written all over it. This is what it means to have a true spirit of giving. I could share other stories like this, but I believe this particular story speaks volumes.

I may have been mentally struggling, but God's favor was apparent. I had family and friends who cared for me. And this particular season, the reason for going to college and the promise I had made to Jesus, was beginning to form.

My first book was being born. I had joined a writing group with Marki, and had written several chapters on the book that had no title. The group helped edit to make it more appealing.

When I researched information about Daddy Frank to add to the book, and shared with him what it was going to be about, he didn't even hesitate as he said call it, *"Time To Come Home."* When a person reads the book, they will see why that is the perfect title.

So the book was born and titled; I had a supporting family and friends; and this season keeps on giving … Jim had found the woman he was going to marry. He went on two dates with Barb and was getting ready to go on his third date when he said, "This is the one!"

This season was certainly filled to the brim with God's blessings.

New Beginnings

Chapter 23

My parents had bought a house and property in Montana. Will and his family were in on the deal. Between them and my folks they bought 100 acres in the mountains of Trego, Montana. It was one of those small towns with a school, a general store, a post office and a fire station/community center. The town could have had a bumper sticker made saying, *"Where the hell is Trego, Montana?"*

Well, it was 13 miles from the town to the property. It was located at the 4,000 mountain foot level. And if you wanted to buy groceries other than what the general store *"Trego Mall"* carried, you had to drive 33 miles into Eureka, and if you wanted to go shopping for clothes or department store products it was a mere 60 miles to Kalispell.

Summer was when I visited the place the first time. I fell in love with the beauty. My parent's property included a large house, which Daddy Frank called his hunting cabin, there was a cabin and an old out house near to the house, and across the road stood a huge old rustic barn. Over by the creek there was a water pump house, and an old shed, which Daddy would use for hunting stuff that I'd rather not share to the non-hunters. On one side of the shed was a garage area. All these buildings were old and rustic made with raw wood and logs, but they were standing firm. The barn appeared as though it could have been blown over by the slightest wind.

Wild flowers and trees filled the hills; there were acres of pasture land (a rancher's dream). The national forest was right behind the property. Talk about picturesque; this property should have made the cover of a magazine.

A mobile home sat on the property near the creek. A home on water front property, how much more perfect does it get? I thought to myself I'd love to live here; it was so peaceful and serene, a majestic place to write a book.

I was no weenie woman; hard work was no stranger to me. I was confident that I could be a care taker for my folk's hunting village. I wanted to live in this tranquil setting, and felt strongly that the Lord wanted me in this place.

So my parents and I were in agreement; I would see them summer and during hunting season and live happily ever after in the mountains of Montana.

The summer of 1995 would bring a new home and new life; I would be a grandmother in the spring – Wow! I must say if there were a stronger word for euphoric, that's how I was feeling – totally in God's favor! "Let's go God!"

Promises in Parts

*God didn't promise a rose garden just yet-
Just some rose buds along the way
to keep a soul burning.
His Word does not promise heaven on
earth just yet –
Only glimpses of it to keep a heart
yearning for Him!*

Close to Paradise

Chapter 24

Will, his mother, Shelly and brother, Ted tried to warn me about the winters. My character is one that challenges the words, "You can't do this, or it will be too hard for you." I had enough self doubt thrown at me as a child. I'd show everyone I could do it. How bad could it get?

The place looked like paradise. The pastures were golden; the sun was warm; the creek was moving and trickling in a calming flow; the wild flowers filled the hills and land; the larch trees were turning orange, yellow and red. I'd never seen these type trees. They looked a lot like they came from the pine family. Standing on the hill behind the property, I admired the incredible scenery.

But reality slowly crept in as I was about to experience my first strange phenomenon.

No one had lived in the house for several months before my folks prepared to move in late summer. So when we entered the house it was a freaky fly

A Plan For You

---

sight; flies, mostly dead, covered the carpet and light fixtures and window sills, the ones struggling to live were in the windows. I never saw so many flies in one place in my life, dead or alive.

We discovered as long as someone lived in the home the problem wasn't such a big deal. We never could figure out why this happened; perhaps they laid eggs in the rope that trimmed the walls. We never knew. So with me living next door and keeping an eye on the home, it was under fly control. And together we made their place comfortable and cozy.

Getting my mobile ready for living in was fun. I put my desk and word processor in front of the window that faced the barn, pasture and mountains behind it. When the sun rose it reflected golden light on the mountain ridge. I was always up before it came up, and before the chickens, as well. I enjoyed hearing Shelly's rooster crow every morning. Her mobile home sat on a cliff about quarter mile from mine.

Preparing for winter was all about having enough wood, making sure the pipes were wrapped, and much more. I chipped right in and earned my keep. We got as ready as we thought necessary, according to our neighbors, who knew well what was to come.

Will and Ted helped Daddy Frank with many projects, mostly Ted, as Will traveled back and forth to Seattle to work. Ted loved Mom's cooking and enjoyed when it was summer time and hunting season so he could spend time with my folks. Shelly joined us for dinner sometimes, too. The snow began to fall; it was so beautiful. Ted taught me how to plow. We had a blazer for plowing that came with the property. It was three miles to the main road, which wasn't all that main, but it was plowed regularly by the big trucks. I learned that you have to drive at least 35 miles per hour to make the snow fly off to the side of the road. It feels like 50 miles per hour in snow. My sister, Sherry rode with me a few times and was impressed, as well as nervous. I felt pleased with myself when I plowed snow during the week, while Ted was gone driving truck.

I was to survive in the mountains alone during my first winter in Montana. With hunting season over, my folks went back home to California; Ted was working; and Will and Shelly were in an unfortunate accident. The truck slid on ice on their way back to the property, leaving Shelly with broken bones. Shelly had to stay in Seattle to recover and to receive necessary Medical care.

If an emergency were to occur on the mountain, a rescue copter would have to come and get you; there was no ambulance service in these mountains. The nearest neighbor, when Shelly and Ted weren't around, was four miles away.

Me and my dog, Storm celebrated Christmas together. I enjoyed watching the snow, cooking a holiday meal, and going for a walk; which would become a big part of our daily agenda. Our two canine neighbors would join us for our four mile walk, as I was watching Shelly and Ted's animals during the week. It was a great time to talk out loud to the Lord. Of course, Shelly was high on my prayer list.

A Plan For You

I didn't mind being alone. A writer appreciates isolation such as this.

But I did look forward to visiting Ted and his girlfriend when they came home for the weekend. Cathy was quiet and sweet, a pleasure to be around. She lived in Whitefish, near Kalispell. When I had to make my 60 mile trip to do super shopping, I'd visit her.

I wore my purple snow boots for six months, even when I drove to town, or the post office. There was no need for shoes when the snow came up past your knees on the property. I drove to the post office three times a week, and then to Eureka twice a month. I always made a list and checked it twice before the long trip to town.

Country music dominated the radio waves. I learned to appreciate country music. The news was almost funny compared to the big city: A cow got hit in the road; a bar room brawl in town; a Jet Ski accident, or a wild animal attack.

I moved along on my book and wrote letters every morning; I chopped kindling and carried wood into my folk's house; kept a fire going to keep the pipes warm in their house. I shoveled snow, and when it was knee deep on the mobile roof, I'd go up and shovel it off for more than three hours, but I did what was necessary. Those were just some of the duties I performed.

I had a pellet stove and oil heat. I had to go to Eureka to get oil for the heater. When the power went out, nothing worked in the mobile. The mountain winds were fierce and knocked the power out often,

A Plan For You

but I was amazed at how fast the power company got it back on. It didn't matter what time or hour, they were quick to get the power restored.

When the temperature dropped below zero, it sucked my breath right out of me. I'd never experienced this type of cold in my life. I did my daily duties regardless: I'd walk to the chicken coop and dig the snow away to get to them; then I'd feed and give them fresh water a few times a day, as the water froze in a matter of minutes. I'd also do the same for the cats; they had a little house with a heating pad inside to keep them warm. The dogs stayed with me during the week.

If I were to get buried in snow, get attacked by a wild animal, or froze to death, it would have been a week before someone would discover I had been eaten or was dead.

Daddy Frank left me some of his guns, in case of wild animals. He showed me how to shoot his guns and explained what type of shooting each one was for. Some of them nearly knocked me on my butt, but I had good training.

I didn't have to use any of them, although, one evening, as I walked back home from dinner with my folks, a wolf ran past me. The coyotes yipped every night like they wanted to kill something; their eerie sound echoed loudly from the pasture only a few hundred feet away. I kept the dogs in with me at night to keep us all safe and warm. And I remembered the news stories about how deadly the cougars and bear were.

I was definitely alone in the wilderness and I wasn't afraid. Knowing all this, I dare anyone to call me a weenie or a sissy now.

Princess Outside of Paradise

Chapter 25

Spring came, the snow melted and the creek turned into a raging river. It came over the ridge right behind my mobile. The surrounding rivers in the neighborhood were extremely high. The pasture was a swamp. The road was so soft that getting stuck in the mud was just as common as getting stuck in the snow. If Ted wasn't around then I wouldn't be going anywhere.

Shelly returned home and I was thankful for her sake and glad to have a neighbor close by again.

I was more excited about my grandchild who was soon to be born. I planned to drive to Seattle to see the new baby right after he or she was born, and after the roads dried up enough to drive on.

Jim and Barb decided to make the birth a surprise. I looked forward to talk with Jim on the phone every week. He kept telling me he wanted a boy. Then on the day the baby was due, he said he hoped it would be a girl. And our little princess, Shayla was born April 23, 1996.

What a blessing to have another girl in the family. No one would take Marcie's place, but it was wonderful to have a girl child in our lives. God makes no mistakes about what He does and how He does it. Shayla was a healthy baby that we adored.

I waited until May, which was almost too long of a wait for this excited Gramma. But the roads were soggy in April and driving out of the mountains would be easier to accomplish in May.

The year Shayla was born was one where snow and avalanches were a major problem on all the Washington State passes. So the snow took longer to melt. May was a better time to travel through Montana, Idaho and Washington.

Shayla was beautiful; thin golden hair, close to bald, hazel eyes (more blue at birth). I saw Jim, Marcie and Barb in her. She was a gift- life is a God given gift. When Jim handed her over to me and I held her for the first time, I had the same spiritual experience as I did when my children were born. But what made this even more supernatural, was my son sweetly and tenderly handed his daughter over to me. The presence of Jesus was there in the room at that miraculous moment. How do I know – I know! There isn't a simple way to explain the presence of Jesus; there's nothing simple about Him.

I dreaded going back to Montana, but that's where I lived and I needed to get back to take care of the property in a new season. So "Gramma, Ice Princess" drove back to paradise, leaving my little princess behind.

Property Problems in Paradise

Chapter 26

The dryer season was much more like the paradise I started out with. The ranchers drove the cattle out in trailers and dropped them off to grange in our neighborhood.

If you didn't want them in the yard, they'd have to be chased off, and the dogs were good for this job. My dog, Storm was a natural at it and looked forward to the command, "Go get em'!"

One summer morning, I was awakened by a black bull making a desperate cry for his cows. I guess he got lost from the heard. My window was opened, so I was startled by what I was hearing and jumped out of bed to see what was making the horrid noise.

"Good Fences make good neighbors" is a very old saying, but is so very true.

With cows, running around eating the flowers, getting into the gardens, not to mention pooping all over the main yards, which took me three days to mow, it was essential to keep them out.

Shelly had a big garden that the cows managed to find. What fences we did have didn't keep them out. When the dogs chased them the cows literally jumped the fences, every one of them. I was amazed.

Easements are another issue in the country. The neighbor that lived four miles away was one of the ranchers that let his cattle loose to grange. He was to build an easement to get to his property instead of him and his hired hands driving right down the middle of our land to get to the other side of his property. Swamp land was the cause for him not being able to come in from the side closest to his ranch.

It was okay when one or two people drove on that easement. But here I am in the middle of nowhere, and I watched many people drive through: logging trucks, wood cutters, hired hands. It was ridiculous. Something was wrong with this busy highway in pasture land.

One evening Ted and I were loading bails of hay on his truck. It was getting late and dark. As we worked, we watched four vehicles go past us. Ted said the old cliché, "This is grand central station out here."

So being that part of the property belonged to Shelly and Ted, we unanimously decided to lock the main gate, which started the war out in the wilderness.

They called the guy that sold us all the property and so did we. The neighbors ended up having to build their own easement, but not without animosity

A Plan For You

toward us. It wasn't very neighborly of us to keep them from driving logging trucks and other big rigs on the dirt road and through the pasture in front of the house. It was stressful then, but I laugh when I relive this time; who would have thought I'd be fighting with neighbors in paradise?

So long Paradise

Chapter 27

The summers in Trego were warmer than Seattle; in fact it was down right hot and I'd cool off in the creek or go swimming in Dickey Lake. Several lakes in Montana are as big as the Puget Sound, for instance, Flat Head.

I didn't get many visitors while living in the big country, but I had it ready for company, especially for my grand daughter. I made my yard like a park. I enjoyed preparing for company to see this beautiful piece of paradise.

Finally, before summer ended, company came from Washington. I was excited to entertain them. Mindy and Percy came and we had barbecues and campfires next to the creek. Ted and Shelly joined us some nights. The sky at night was big and filled with stars; they appeared to be closer than I had ever seen any stars - a breathtaking view. The saying that Montana is Big Sky Country is absolute truth.

A Plan For You

During the day, we ventured out and saw property I hadn't seen yet.

I'd lived there a year and this was the only company to visit me from back home. When they left, I was sad.

Approaching hunting season, my folks would soon be coming. I had this to look forward to. When they arrived, I had more company than anticipated, as Sister Sherry came with them, and she brought her Cockatoo. Their house was filled with life, a little loud at times. I was glad for my peaceful domain next door. I had Storm dog and Koa, my cockatiel; her noise was tolerable. But Sherry's bird was extremely loud, but very funny. He could imitate Stevey Wonder and Michael Jackson at command.

My folks stayed for three months. It was a good long visit. We had a wonderful Christmas, a season sprinkled with comical memories, and showered with a non-comical snow fall. The memories make my heart both smile and laugh.

Mom got her white Christmas. A record year snow hit us hard. Then there was the perfect Christmas tree that Daddy Frank almost killed himself to get for her. He and I went together and we eyeballed a tree that fit her description. It was located down an incline piled with snow. He started the chain saw and headed down the ravine and fell with the saw blade rotating.

After we realized he was okay, we laughed out loud at what we were doing to get mom the perfect tree.

A Plan For You

Speaking of ravines, here's a story about hunting where two deer didn't get away. Daddy hauled the smaller one to the house; then had me go with him to help get "the big one that didn't get away." It laid about ½ mile away and was located down a ravine approximately 25 or more feet. What a "Mountain Mama" I had become. Daddy had emphazema and it was too much for him to lug a big deer like this one alone. We both pulled it up the steep incline; then I dragged it with a harness back to the house. I felt like Daddy's son. He was proud of me for what I was able to do, but mostly for my faith in the Lord. Daddy was bold where he stood for Jesus, and I admired him for that reason. Since Marcie's death, Mom and he had grown more in Jesus. But Daddy was totally dedicated and made no bones about it. The family knew where he stood. His mission was to teach others the simple message of salvation; especially to his family; which would be a constant challenge.

And speaking of challenge, back on the ranch; Daddy, Ted and I tried to keep up with the plowing of the heavy snow fall. But it over took us twice, and we had to pay someone with a big rig to plow us out.

This was the year that Sherry was impressed with my snow plowing ability. I had some practice from the previous year. But this year was making me an expert.

This was also the heaviest snow fall to occur in this area in 100 years. Go figure. Sherry's nick name is Murphy, because everything gets screwed up around her life. But this was my life as well.

A Plan For You

After Mom and Daddy went back home, Sherry and I entertained one another to keep from going bonkers in the snow. I continued to walk four miles in it every day.

God has a wonderful way of making every season pleasing to the human eye, but may He forgive me when I say that I had seen enough snow to last me a life time.

March came and there was still snow on the ground and a couple of feet of it remained on the roofs. Sherry and I decided to do something fun. We had a Luau in the snow. We put on our shorts, went out in the snow and took pictures of ourselves drinking are tropical drinks with little umbrellas in them. Then we quickly put our warmer clothes back on, and I barbecued Elk meat to go with the special occasion.

Not too long after this time, we talked it over and I wanted to go back to Washington and she wanted to back to her home town. I missed my son and wanted to watch my granddaughter grow. She was almost one year old. I lived in Montana nearly two years and they hadn't come for a visit. I wanted to be more a part of Shayla's life.

I spent much time in prayer about this decision. My four mile walks with my dog was my prayer time; only this time I needed a way to get back and get my life restarted. I'd need a place to stay for me and my dog, and I needed a job making at least $10 dollars an hour to get back up and running in Seattle.

I made arrangements to stay with Marty and her husband, as she had a fenced back yard with a dog and an extra room that I could stay in until I found a place.

So it was a done deal. Ted would take a load of stuff in his truck and haul my car on a trailer. He planned to take it to Will's shop and home. We packed Sherry's stuff and my dog and the two birds in her vehicle. I didn't think we were going to get off the property, as the melted snow on the roads had turned the path to mush and mud. Ted got his truck with my stuff in it stuck and had to get his big grader to pull it out.

So when we were on smooth solid road, I said, "Goodbye paradise."

God Doesn't Miss a Beat

Chapter 28

I requested what I believed I needed and nothing more. I was easily pleased and my requests were simple. I needed a job that would pay enough to rent a place and be suitable for me and Storm dog. I wasted no time finding a job. I got my old job back cleaning Will's shop. Mindy was happy as we could spend time together again. She was faithful to call, write and visit me while in Montana.

I went into the nursing home I had worked in eight years prior. My old boss was still there. In spite of our differences in character, she was glad to see me and I got a job in activities for $7.50 an hour.

My friends Cindy and Gertrude were still there. Cindy shared the heart ache she endured over losing Ralph in detail. She suffered and drank to the point of nearly killing herself and that's what she wanted to occur. But God intervened, and in His unique way He reminded her that promiscuous behavior could bring fatal health problems; therefore Cindy

A Plan For You

realized she cared about living again. It was a long process getting to that point, however. But God does whatever it takes, because that's how much He loves us individually.

And speaking of whatever it takes, in doing the math, the two jobs gave me the money that I requested. Plus Marty's friend had a duplex for rent with a fenced yard at a rent price I could afford.

I didn't request of the Lord that the job be close to work, but I did ask for a place out and away from the crowded areas. And again, He heard my every prayer!

It took some readjusting to drive in heavy traffic, to wait in lines at grocery stores, and to smell exhaust in the air. Plus, I had to relearn not to wave at passing cars in my neighborhood. I was back in a world of commercial and chaos. The news was filled with horror stories; drive by shootings and murders. Not like mountain news; bar room brawls, snowmobile accidents and running over a cow. After waving at a few surprised neighbors, Common sense told me, "Don't wave."

I was home and was convinced when I was with Jim and Shayla. Barb and Jim were good parents. I appreciated that Barb made me important to Shayla's life.

I had so much fun, singing and dancing, playing games, watching kid's movies over and over again. What a blessing to have the opportunity and the maturity to experience times I would treasure and save in my memory bank. I wish I could have had times like these with my children. But there is a big difference between being a teen mother and a 40 something grandmother.

After getting settled and making my home comfortable, I got back into writing *Time To Come Home*. This book was five years in the making and was Seven years away from completion. But God's timing is perfect! And I'm on His time line.

My life was being put in order by way of Jesus. And the fact that I was willing to take the necessary steps, every beat was made possible. It is absolutely true that "Nothing is impossible through Christ our Lord!"

Into Jesus

My pain is a path
that leads
to promise
to peace
into the presence
of Jesus
My tears are a trench
that flows
through troubles
through trials
into the river of life
My heaviness is a hope
that brings
my hurt
my heart
into the loving arms
of Jesus

Adjustments and Trials

Chapter 29

I am not going to tell you that aligning with God made my life problem free. I believe it would be wrong for any Christian to tell you that. The Bible does not tell us life is going to be hunky dory for believing; only that it will be easier to get through by faith and that Jesus is always with you, "*I will never leave you nor forsake you.*"

If we had a life with perfection and no needs, there would be no need for Jesus. We aren't in heaven. And you may want to thank Him for your trials and troubles.

> James 1:2 – 4: *Consider it a pure joy whenever you face trials of many kinds, because you know that the testing of your faith develops perseverance. Perseverance must finish its work so you may be mature and complete, not lacking anything.*

Leave Your Mother

I experienced heartache when I knew that the Bible says a son must leave his mother and make his wife priority. I had so much of Jim's love and many years with him that I had a big adjustment to make. I was humble and understood what God's Word says about marriage. But I must say it was hard to step down from the high position that I had been in Jim's life. Although I had lived in the wilderness alone for nearly two years, I felt lonely taking the back seat to my son. I suppose this is a natural response for most mothers, but losing Marcie connected Jim and I more closely than most mother and son.

Although I was in the back seat, I was pleased to see my son be a good father who took priority in providing for his family. He loved his family and took his position as husband and father serious.

I prayed to Jesus that Jim would know where his wisdom and his strong loving characteristics came from. God gave Jim a fine example of a family provider in Daddy Frank. Jim admired his Grandpa.

Jim was an observer and gained insight when he watched family and friends make mistakes that messed up their lives or killed them. He chose not to go in any of those directions. If only I would have taken some lessons in that area. I had to be tasting waters outside of the boundaries, experiencing things first-hand and getting soak and wet in the process.

Although painful, the adjustment was well worth seeing my son become a strong and loving young man.

Come Home Mark

My brother Mark had struggled with troubled waters most of his life. He went in and out of sobriety. I recall a time when I was visiting my family in California when Mark appeared happy in Mom's eyes. Mark had been sober for two years at that time, had a good job, a nice automobile, and a good woman. We were having a family barbecue.

Mom made the comment, "Isn't it nice to see Mark so happy?"

"I'm not happy," Mark sharply replied.

No one responded, but I never forgot that statement. Mark had a penetrated sadness that not even God could reach; although He was with Mark and placed caring people in his life, Mark always felt unlovable. Our abusive childhood didn't help him with that negative thought process. Satan worked my brother over. The bald- headed man (Satan) hung out in our bedrooms as children and Mark was haunted by him as an adolescent, and I'm positive, well on into his adult years.

I had my last vision of the bald- headed man when I was a young table dancer; living a life that pleased Satan and displeased God. (See story in *Time to Come Home*). This was not my last encounter with Satan, as he came to me as other characters to bring fear my way as aforementioned. My faith sustained me, but my brother had very weak faith.

Mark struggled mostly with alcohol, but had also been heavy into drugs. Alcohol was easier and cheaper to get. Mark became violent when drinking.

Mom said he acted just like Dad. He would fight anyone in his path, including his own family. He pushed people away with this negative behavior.

He spent time in Jail for many of his fights in bars. Hurting people was his main focus when drinking. I suppose that stemmed from his bottled up hurt.

When he was out on his binges, he often called Mom and cried like a child and would say, "I'm scared Mom. Please let me come home."

My folks loved Mark, and were willing to help him when he was sober. He could stay with them and work. He went to church and Bible study with them. He accepted the Lord as his Savior more than once. He did as a boy and few times as a man because he was desperate to be loved.

When Mark and I talked on the phone, we talked about Jesus. Jesus was important to him. But he seemed to believe he wasn't good enough to be loved by God or anyone. I had a hard time convincing him otherwise. He talked about his friend from church that he worked with. God was always placing Christians in his life. Daddy Frank was a strong and bold example.

Another two years of sobriety went by and all appeared well with Mark on the outside. He was working, helping Daddy Frank around the home and working with a Christian man doing various jobs.

But Mark had a deep-seeded hatred for himself that he couldn't undue. He couldn't intercept the truth about Jesus' forgiveness being a done deal for him for the asking, and that He loved Mark like he was the only person in the world.

A Plan For You

Christmas 1998 was approaching and Mark was growing restless. Mom called to share sad news that Mark had taken off again.

Mom shared that they were watching Television together. Mark was sober, but his remarks weren't sobering to hear.

"Mom, I can't live like this anymore; I just have to go back."

Mom knew very well what he was indicating. He meant that he was going back to San Jose to resume his unstable hellish life of drinking.

Mom wanted to say something to help him want to stay with her and Daddy.

"We love you Mark."

"You always say that; I want to hear you say, 'I love you Mark!'"

She responded, "I love you Mark!"

He grabbed a peace of paper and pen and wrote the words, "My mom says she loves me."

Mom is not sure where the note went, but believes Mark stuck in his pocket.

Early Christmas Eve morning he headed back to the life of being a drunkard.

The New Year got off to a shocking start: The phone rang at my folks house interrupting their dinner. Daddy Frank answered the call. Mom said she knew by listening and watching Daddy's response. His friend from San Jose said, "Mark's dead."

His body was taken for an autopsy, which revealed his gastro intestine exploded, killing him instantly. He drank until he passed out then he blacked out for good on January 4, 1999.

A Plan For You

I got my call that night and just cried so loud it sounded like I was screaming. I hurt so much for my brother and because of our hurtful past understood his life struggle. I recalled some of his beatings as a boy. I bawled for the little boy that yearned for love and couldn't receive any.

I was thankful for the knowledge, truth and faith I had in Jesus. My heart was crushed that Mark couldn't get beyond his painful past and know the love Jesus always had for him.

I called and talked to Mrs. Teshera. She said she remembered the cute little boy Mark was and we shared sweet memories of him. I thanked her and God for her and Reverend, for the example of Jesus they were to us as children. She was comforting to talk with, but I was all messed up inside. I wished I could have comforted Mark and let him know how much I loved him. He needed to know he was loved in the worst way and it killed him.

While grieving, God put this thought in my heart. Jesus came for Mark at his death bed and said, "Come home Mark; your struggle is over." Mark knows he's loved, at last!

Falling

Once again I come to you
asking for forgiveness
asking for mercy
I have fallen
yet again
one more time
Once again you forgive me
Once again you give me mercy
No matter how many times I fall
you will be there to pick me up
yet again
one more time!

Sucked in

Chapter 30

My friends Mindy and Percy had a Harley-Davidson, as did Jim and Midge. I became acquainted with Jim and Midge through Mindy and Percy. Jim went to school with Percy, plus they were next door neighbors. Jim's wife, Midge was just learning to ride a motorcycle at that time.

The summer of '99 was a warm and good summer for riding, and for communing with fellow motorcycle riders on Highway 99. Mindy would invite me to Taco Thursday nights, where the parking lot was layered with 500 motorcycles or more.

I was right at home in the midst of these people, and the sound of Harley-Davidsons pumped up the beat of my heart. I was sucked into these machines.

From riding my bicycle all over the place as a kid; to riding on the back of Harley-Davidsons; then coming to Washington and getting back into the motorcycle scene, it was becoming evident that I was meant to be in the wind.

A Plan For You

Most of these riders were there for the purpose of getting together. They didn't have any other agenda. Some Club members showed up, but things stayed peaceful for the most part.

On my 50th birthday Mindy gave me a birthday party at Taco Thursday. My son even came. What a loud and exciting night.

My friends introduced me to Barry. He was cute; he was a small man, about my height; wore a long pony tail. Although he was younger than me his hair was silver streaked. Barry had come from a background of drugs and alcohol and living a wild biker life. He had been clean and sober for seven years. When he meant me, he was attending A.A. meetings and had a good job at Boeing.

He asked me on a day date. He was a gentleman to me. We went for a ride out in the country. I was being lured in by his kindness, and ignored all the warning signs: he was recently divorced; he had a spoiled child-like temperament; and allergies to just about everything. He tolerated my Storm dog. Although I kept her clean, he said she stunk.

God was trying to communicate to me, but I was being lured in for the fact, Barry rode a Harley-Davidson, spoiled and adored me; anything I mentioned that I liked was mine. And I believed that he loved God, as I had seen the Bible on his coffee table when I visited. He talked about finding a church to go to. He was reading the *Left Behind* book series. So in my mind God was cool about us.

But all this did was put an unsettling confirmation in my mind to sin. I made up excuses believing God had put a Christian biker in my life.

Barry treated me like a princess. I became more blind-sighted and awe struck, and I enjoyed being the center of attention. I don't recall ever being put on a pedestal by any man.

I continued to pray about us, and tried to make our relationship right in God's eyes. I moved in with him, knowing it was wrong. But the adoration took my main focus off of God.

It broke my heart to get rid of Storm dog. I gave her to a wonderful family that had a fenced acre of land with another dog to play with. I feel bad to this day about giving her up for a man I only thought that I loved.

I stopped writing *Time To Come Home*. I built my world around Barry, just exactly as he desired.

The first year was like a fairy tale story. My world was Barry centered, it was about him, our friends, and it had no Deena life outside of Barry's world. We took rides on the motorcycle, went on runs with friends and it was exciting.

I was able to ignore the temperament and control, because I was being adored, and that made up for the uncalled for, "Your not doing that right," or drawing out an argument that I didn't see coming, nor could I figure why or where or what it stemmed from. So on occasion, my old self came forth and I told him where to go in response.

Barry wasn't physically abusive and, of course if he had been, with my old track record he would have been abused by me and left before he hit the floor.

After awhile being cherished took back seat, as I was beginning to open my eyes and see the reality of what God had been trying to warn me about.

I realized I missed the freedom and independence I had outside of Barry's world and our world. I had never had anyone tell me to watch how long I talk on the phone to my mother; just one of many examples of his need to CONTROL.

I began to feel smothered and very depressed; the kind that left me without energy; plus fearful as I knew big changes were about to occur. And I had night mares:

Marcie sat on a linoleum floor in a state hospital. She had on a night gown; I was mentally sick and being led by nurses, one on each side of me. They wouldn't let me go to Marcie. I cried like a wounded child. The nurses led me to a giant crib and I put my thumb in my mouth and wet the bed.

I sat straight up in the bed and screamed, then laid back down and returned sleeping. Barry yelled at me for screaming, as I had scared him, but I don't remember the screaming part.

I rode in a big black Cadillac with red leather interior. I got trapped and couldn't open the doors or windows. Barry was in the car and wouldn't let me out. I was devastated and trapped. And that was what was happening to me in real life.

Barry didn't see himself as having a control, anger, or self-centered problem.

I had come from being an independent God-Centered woman of more than 11 years to a kept woman, and I was screaming inside. But this time I didn't run away - I tried to salvage the relationship by asking Barry to go to counseling with me. He responded, "You get counseling if you want, I don't have a problem." And that attitude was our major problem.

So I did just that; I went to a Christian Counselor that my coworker friend, Ann knew. Ann was going to school to get her Master's Degree in Christian Counseling and referred me to her friend. Ann was listening and helping me through with her knowledge, but felt I needed to talk to a professional, as we were connected as friends. Not only were we work friends, we were about to become long-term neighbors as well.

I went to the counselor, explained everything and she suggested I move out immediately, that the relationship wasn't healthy. She told me straight up, "living with him was a sin in God's eyes." In my heart, I always knew this to be true. I made no more excuses.

I went to Mindy and Percy's place to stay for the night, and called Barry and asked him to allow me to move my stuff out while he was at work. He agreed, but was puzzled in response. But it had to be this way. I knew it was God's will.

My son helped me move and let me stay with him for a month until I found an apartment down the street from my work place and Ann's neighborhood.

A Plan For You

I'm not going to say that I was relieved. I struggled with pain and forced myself not to contact Barry. Several times I picked up the phone and God spoke to my heart, "Put it down." There was something about being adored that was hard to shake loose. I prayed for Barry to get into the truth and Word of Jesus, but he chose a destructive path. He started drinking after seven years of sobriety, met a gal less than two months after I left, moved in with her, married her and it ended in another divorce.

Eventually my wounds were healed and a good lesson was learned. I give all the credit to Jesus. I was now on His path and moving forward with His Plan for my life.

Hearts Beat On

Chapter 31

When my son's heart broke, so did mine. I had recovered from my breakup with Barry. But Jim was about to go through his heartache. I was his ear with unconditional passion. My son and I had a close connection that began to grow strong after Marcie died. We talked about anything and everything. No communication gaps with us.

Barb merely fell out of love with him and even with his suggestion to go to counseling; her mind was set on divorce. They were able to be good friends and were civil and fair about the separation, and they had mutual love and concern for Shayla's well-being.

But to see my son's heart torn, broke mine. As a mother I wanted to fix him – kiss his cheek and make the pain go away.

I listened and even when the divorce set in to stage... anger, and he reminded me of what a poor example I was for marriage and relationships, I stayed loving and calm. I know from experience what people do when they are in pain; they lash out in different ways. If it made my son feel better to blame me for his divorce, then so be it.

I knew that he didn't mean what he was saying and knew that he loved me. I prayed everyday for my son's healing, and I even sacrificed myself by asking God to give his pain to me, because I could handle it better – whatever I needed to do to make him feel good about his life. I prayed my son would open his heart to a personal relationship with Jesus. And still do so. I pray that Christians surround him. He listens to what I know about Jesus and appears curious, but his heart isn't opened wide enough. And I do like so many mamas, hope and pray that my prayers will save him, but the truth is only Jesus can save his soul. But I trust and know Jesus has not missed a single prayer!

As I said, time heals wounds, but Jesus really does the trick. Jim bought a new home and he enjoyed fixing it up and spending time with Shayla, and his heart was on the mend. I didn't realize it at the time, but Coach Mike was still in Jim's life. He is and has been a strong Christian man since my son was a high school freshman in wrestling. And his new neighbor, Sandy was a good neighbor and friend for him. She and I became close friends and even when she moved away, we stayed in touch. We saw the *Passion of the Christ* when it first hit the theatres and cried together and talked about our love for Jesus. We read the *Left Behind* series and discussed the coming of Christ. I was thankful for Sandy being my son's friend and to see then and now that he is surrounded by Christians.

A Plan For You

I was always a part of Shayla's life, but more involved in it when Jim had her for the weekends. She grew to be pretty - hazel eyes and golden hair, and to be athletic, like her dad and grandma. Barb was athletic, too, but Jim and I were hyper and we channeled our hyperactivity into dancing, running and other athletic activities. Although Shayla wasn't as hyper as we were, she was most definitely highly active, and she enjoyed being involved in sports. Her interests were in playing soccer and running. I took pride, as did Jim and Barb in watching her play; although I didn't get as worked up as they did while yelling supporting commands from the sidelines. I laughed inside at their loving way of cheering her on.

Although it was hurtful and awkward for all concerned at first, Jim and Barb's mutual love was ever present on Shayla's behalf. She had no negativity thrown in her face – only love; which is a sign of strong and sacrificing love. And Jim has this kind of love for Shayla.

I made a better Grandmother than a Mom; I made so many mistakes, the kind you don't want to write home about, but I wrote a whole book about. But God has forgiven me and blest me with my son, who is wise and also forgives me. He genuinely loves me and his daughter. And I will continue to pray for his heart to be open to the love that Jesus has for him, and that he will know he has been gifted because of the love God has for him. May he tap into the love and gifts and surrender his heart to Jesus!

God is in the business of healing broken hearts and he healed us both and our hearts beat on!

I follow the Son

As I ride into the sunrise in the wee hours
I feel the presence of Jesus all around me!
As the wind touches my face and
whirls my hair
He invigorates me!
As the fragrance of the forest
penetrates my nostrils
He refreshes me!
As I ride into the heart of the day
The sun shines brightly over my head
He comforts me!
As I approach the magnificent ocean
At the end of my ride
I see the golden red sun
in its glory!
As I watch the colorful reflections
across the water
He gives me joy!
And I am reminded why
I follow the Son!

Premonitions & Priming

Chapter 32

Time may be said to heal all wounds, but staying focused on Jesus really does the trick! I typed away on *Time To Come Home* and continued to write poems for Jesus.

I served him by caring for residents in nursing homes. I seemed to get the Sunday schedule to work, so I fellowshipped with the volunteers who came in to conduct Bible Studies and Church Services. Godly people were always put in my path and I befriended many of them.

Now that my focus was back on Jesus, I heard from Him in interesting ways: I woke up one morning and before I could put my feet on the floor, I kept repeating *"Barnes and Noble, Barnes and Noble"*, and I couldn't figure out why. So when I got up with these words still phased into my mind and coming out of my mouth, I thought that's where I am suppose to go get a new lounge chair. I had just moved in next door to Ann and needed a new chair. (Talk

A Plan For You

about funny) I wasn't a reader, but I could write and I didn't even know that *Barnes and Noble* was a major book store, and I was writing a book.

My coworker, Denise straightened me out when I told her about the voices in my head. We both laughed so hard when I told her I thought *Barnes and Noble* was a furniture store. God has a sense of humor. And this story is being made miraculous in my ignorance.

Then another morning I awoke in the wee hours of the morning, like always. I lay in bed and visualized myself riding down a highway on a Harley-Davidson; no one was on the road. As I look back now, I see that it was yellow (my favorite color). I was happy in the vision. When I got up, I went straight to the processor and wrote the aforementioned poem. I sent it to the Christian Crusaders motorcycle group, and they printed in their section of a motorcycle magazine. I was excited for myself and felt strongly that I would be living this poem someday.

As I walked to work that May morning, I was in awe of my surroundings; the new vivid green growth, a soft breeze gently rustling the new born leaves and touching my face, spring flowers of various colors were all along my path, and birds singing as if they were singing just for me. I could have walked for hours that morning, as I knew I was in the very presence of Jesus. As I approached the building to go in, something made me look up to the sky and a flock of white doves silently flew over my head. The Holy Spirit made a strong presence in my core being.

I smiled in awe! I knew I was to ride in the wind with Jesus someday.

I told my coworker friends, and my other coworker friend, Gail who would sooner than I knew be a big part of my dream. I told them all that I was going to get a Harley-Davidson, and mentioned I was going to ride from book store to book store and sign autographs to my book! (If you're going to dream big, go all the way). And as readers have read, I know when God places something in my heart, there's no doubt in my statement. Like the time when Brandy was shocked when I said, "I'm going to college and I'm going to write a best seller." Brandy responded, "You scare me when you do that." Brandy had seen me accomplish many goals in our long years of friendship.

I connected with Gail because we had much in common. She used to ride a Harley-Davidson in her youth and ran with biker people. She had a bike in her garage and planned to ride it again. I said, "We can ride together when I get my bike."

Gail had a no nonsense exterior, but was soft on the inside. She had a heart as big

… Okay, I'll leave out the cliché. I could see in her heart. I enjoyed talking to her and we quickly connected as friends. I could trust her and talk about anything, and Jesus was **all right** with her. I had no idea where this friendship was heading and as she always said, "God has a reason for everything." And He had a good reason for our friendship. Our job was becoming unstable and many of us went to other jobs. Two years would pass before we would meet up again.

May and June have become months where miracles occurred in my life: *I saw the doves fly over my head; I went to a Taco Thursday with friends to find the publication of my poem in the magazine; I earned the Scholastic Achievement Award in Journalism in May; published copies of Time to Come Home would be delivered to me in May; I got my motorcycle endorsement in June and the surprise of my life on Marcie's birthday:*

Sonshine, my yellow Sportster; which was in my price range, had low miles, and the perfect color; I know Marcie and Jesus were there with me. And when I turned over the ignition I was thrilled. Sonshine echoed loudly with sweet rhythm to my ears and shook the foundation - okay, the building. Don't forget about the Barnes and Noble and book signing brain implants that I know are to transpire in God's mysterious fashion and so on ...

That's just a few miracles that God had blest me, but other months hold miracle memories as well. God's in the business of blessing His children.

Ridin' Up Front

Father,
Keep me humble
never too confident
never too independent
Let me remember
to keep Jesus
ridin' up front!
Keep me focused
never looking away
never turning away
Let me remember
to keep Jesus
ridin' up front!
Keep me rejoicing
Always smiling for you
never forgetting
to keep Jesus
ridin' up front!

Gettin' On It!

Chapter 33

Stubborn is my first name; don't tell me I can't do something because I'll have to prove you wrong. My friends Percy and Mindy and Jim and Midge told me to get a smaller bike for a year to get comfortable with riding before getting a Harley – Davidson. That suggestion was not an option, as I took the training course to get my dream bike and that's just what I did.

Gettin' in the wind was a big challenge on Sonshine because she had much more power than those training bikes with 250 ccs; she had 1200 ccs. She weighed close to 500 pounds and I definitely noticed the difference.

So here I go… fallin' down in the wind. Yep, I dropped her four times, got in a wreck and nearly quit the whole bike thing. But I was much tougher than that. And God had plans for my riding. Like just about everything in my life, I had to learn the hard way, but then I'd only get stronger and better

A Plan For You

and stand firm in the wind. After all, remember the childhood I came from: you fall down, you don't cry and you get back on the horse, or you'll get slapped around.

Most of my learning was from self riding. I did some riding with Midge, and some riding with the four of us as a group, and I rode to some Taco Thursdays with them.

I rode over to say hello to Percy one morning, just to take Sonshine out for some more practice. Mindy was at work and she was okay with me stopping to say hello and to go on a long ride with her husband. Her commanding words to him were, "you better keep an eye on her!" Never mind that an attractive woman would be riding with him for the day. My friend trusted me 100 percent, and learning to ride was my only focus.

I had 79 miles under my belt, and I was raring to go out to Spanaway with Percy to see his brother and to visit the cemetery where Marcie was buried, which was located down the street from his brother's place. I had wanted to do this since I got the bike. So away we went. I was nervous being out of my comfort territory, but I managed to keep up with Percy, but with Mindy's command echoing in his ear, he rode easy for my sake. When we arrived I was relieved, and said, "Thank you, Jesus." I never rode without praying first, during and after.

Our visit was over, so we got on our bikes to go to the cemetery. I turned out of the driveway and hit gravel, and yes, went down. Some young men (young mean men) down the road laughed and called me names like, "stupid, Blank" and other piercing curse names. With the helmet and goggles on they couldn't tell I was a woman. They had a field day with my failure and my old self was about to run up the road and punch them out and give them a taste of their own medicine, and call them some deserving names. But God held my tongue.

I was scared, angry, embarrassed all at once. I wanted to quit riding right then. Percy helped me pick the bike up and said, "It's a good thing you got the crash bars." The crash bars protected the tank, and only a tail light was broken. I had skinned knees, hands, elbows and a sore body, and that was with leathers on. But my bike was okay. And in the biker world, this appears to be more important, as long as you don't get killed. Percy sensed that I was freaked and thought I was going to say," let's leave my bike here and go get my truck." But I shocked him. "Let's go; let's just go!"

Visiting the gravesite with Sonshine didn't have the peaceful affect I had anticipated. But I accomplished the mission set before me that day. Truth be known, Marcie is in heaven with Jesus and the cemetery is where I left her fleshly body. It's a human thing to visit where we leave our loved ones bodies. But I can bring a bouquet of flowers home to honor her just as well.

I kept getting on Sonshine and practicing and moved out of my comfort zone and eventually became more comfortable riding for Jesus!

My friends Midge and Gail had been riding with their husbands and advanced quicker than me and were good riders, but we all have stories to tell about our beginning days of riding. And I learned the hard way and by myself and became determined and with Jesus riding up front I'm on my way to the mission he has set before me!

I placed the mark of Jesus on my motorcycle and jacket by using my, *I follow the Son,* logo across the top of a sunshine with a cross in the middle of the back of my jacket; then I invested in a custom paint job of the tank. This master piece was done by a Christian man who does custom paint work for Harley – Davidson. He painted a cross with a flaming sun rays on each side; the name of Jesus was carefully crafted down the center of the tank. I always see Jesus' name when I ride. Everything I do in life is for Jesus and about Jesus!

I Know that I Know

*Being with Jesus is not a promise of days
without suffering
The pains are going to be
There are blessings in the midst of the
raging winds
His very presence evolves in my heart
I know that I know,
that He is God!
Jesus gives me days of joy to
remind me of His undying love
and days of pain to strengthen my character
He prepares me for wicked worldly roads
ahead
I know that I know,
that He is God!
I praise the name of Jesus
His joy is present in my soul
no matter the circumstances
good or bad
I know that I know
that He is my Lord and Savior!
Amen*

Faithful Fathers

Chapter 34

Eventually all of my work friends were in other jobs, and Mickey my Director, and Denise (the *Barnes and Noble* revealer) would refer me to the next brand new, just opened facility for Alzheimer's/Dementia residents. I was excited for the change. And I did my job well, to the point of being recognized as a worker who went above and beyond, and I won the first award in this building. It was an honor, but I was deeply sad that day as the night before my mom was so devastated with her health condition that she took enough of her prescription drugs to knock her out and land her in the crisis ward.

After the second serious operation on her stomach, both operations nearly taking her life, she found herself completely dependent upon Sherry and Daddy Frank for just about everything outside of bed. Daddy Frank felt she would improve faster if she were at home. A hospital bed was set up in the living room. He did anything that needed doing;

A Plan For You

even wiping her rear. I call this total dedication. His focus and faith was all about Mom's recovery. He spent hours in prayer for her and when she'd speak negative, he'd talk Jesus back at her. Marcie's death brought stronger faith in Jesus to Daddy, Mom and me. Daddy's faith was bold and firm; I admired the way he believed. Everyone around him knew where he stood for Jesus. Unfortunately, the rest of the family didn't follow Jesus or take after Daddy Frank, but Daddy was my hero.

This tragedy hurt his heart, as he believed wholeheartedly that Mom would be healed, but mom didn't have that same faith. Her faith was weak and her condition didn't help the situation. The fact that she was helpless made her feel useless and a burden.

Daddy's faith won out and Mom was healed and fixing him dinner again and they returned to church and I wish I could say, "They lived happily ever after." But praises and halleluiahs were in order! Our Father God rewarded us both for a job well done and for serving Him!

God's Girls

Chapter 35

I met some Christian nurses in the new facility. We were all attracted to one another like bees to a humming bird feeder. Renee and Windy were a blessing to be around.

I enjoyed being around people who loved Jesus, and no matter where I worked we always seemed to find one another, but not by chance or happenstance, but by God Himself!

A sweeping out of coworkers began to take place. Corporate wanted to make changes to bring in more residents and, of course, profit. So they brought in a whole new team, several with the new age belief system, crystals, the teaching of self-hypnosis, etc. But they also came with some good ideas, like making the place more home-like. My thought was, these residents are older and are confused and come from the "old time religion" era.

I kept quiet, except to talk to Renee and Windy who both felt this was not good.

A Plan For You

The changes were insane; everyday someone was quitting or rumors were they were going to be fired. The new boss was aggressive, earning the nick name, "Ice Princess."

Mickey's position changed to Human Resources and Denise became the Activity Director, which made me glad, as she made me in charge of the Day Care. I enjoyed the job. After spending seven years working with Mickey and Denise, we knew one another's strengths weaknesses and idiosyncrancies and we accepted one another and worked well together.

Mickey was intelligent and book learning, speaking and writing were her strengths. She edited T*ime To Come Home* before the final manuscript went to the publisher, as did Ann, who had since become my next door neighbor, as I moved in to the duplex next to her.

Satan comes in many disguises and he's got his mission, and that is to destroy the faith of Christians, and bring them down any way he can. He already has the unconfessed sinners where he wants them, so he works harder to get Christians to give up their faith and curse God.

Windy was bold for Jesus and felt it was important that the owners know about the inside shenanigans; then she was fired, but was hired somewhere better where she could use her God-given talents – she stood firm. Denise quit and moved into a better position as well, before she was to get fired for some reason – there was none - but rumor was they were thinking something up. Other good employees quit and were talking of quitting. Political bull was evident.

A Plan For You

When Denise left, they hired a fresh out of college man of 21 years, who hooked up with the other 21 year old activity staff, of who sided with the administrator to go for me next. I mentioned to Corporate who visited the facility for the purpose of finding out why there was so many unhappy staff that there was a lack of communication and back stabbing games going on. I also mentioned that I had lost my position as head of the Day Care, and had became victim to inexperienced leadership. Somehow that truth got back to the "Ice Princess."

I was pulled in her office and falsely fired; meaning she made lies up and wrote them down after I had already signed the sheet. I signed the sheet, as she said, "It doesn't mean you agree, just that you received it." And truth be known, I was so stressed by the poor treatment and by watching unhappy people be fired and leaving in droves, that I wanted a reason to get out of that joke of a place.

Being falsely accused, and being in a stressful setting where you know you're not welcome, puts a damper on the spirit and I went into a depression, what else, another bad depression. Being falsely accused and rejected really stinks – I mean hurts, and who knows best about rejection and false accusations, but Jesus, who suffered all of this and more. Anything we suffer, he already dealt with it. He identifies.

I was out of work for six weeks. Being Christmas time, this was not the best season to be without a job; but God is faithful all the time: Renee kept in touch and sent me her tithing money of a few hundred dollars; Jodee bought me some gifts to give to my granddaughter, (I recall when I did the same for her kids on my credit card on one of her poor Christmases); Daddy Frank and Mom sent money to see me through; and neighbor and friend, Ann, who had sense then received her Master's in Christian Counseling, consoled me, and helped me out with food and gas money so I could go apply for jobs. Reverend (Mrs. Teshera) and Pastor James were consistent at emailing comforting words. And Christmas 2004, I finished *Time to Come Home* and the manuscript was ready to send to the publisher. Wow – that's God!

Avenger

Chapter 36

God is the avenger, not us – "Vengeance is mine says the Lord!"

I was pretty broken by the injustice, but God saw me through with loving people. So as not to bore you, and to make the story a story, I did not mention all who were of support of me.

I felt compelled to give Gail a call; who was about to play an enormous role in God's next Plan. I was looking for work and was wondering if there were any openings in her facility, which was a sister facility of the one I was fired from. I had talked with human resources and was told if I wanted to work for another related company that there was no reason why I couldn't do so.

Gail was glad to hear from me, and yes, there was an activity position opening up very soon. I applied and was hired right away. And another surprise in this next scene was Cindy was working there, and her office was just across the hall. She would also be a comfort to me for the next storm that was just about to blow in. God is something else!

The Activity Director was glad to have my experience and skill. I felt as though I was right where I belonged. I wasn't bothered at all by being fired from a sister facility. I felt avenged by God. He placed me where I would be appreciated and highly favored. The "Ice Princess" and the 21 year old club were all fired.

Moral to the story, "Don't mess with God's girl!"

Another Miracle in May

Chapter 37

Gail and my friendship became stronger. We rode our motorcycles together and shocked many staff and residents. We were the talk of the facility. I gave her the nick name: "Gale Rider," which goes quite well with "Sonshine Rider." Plus, if you knew Gail, it's a fitting name. We recalled when we talked about me getting a Harley, and that we'd ride together, and here it was in God's Plan all along! Another interesting factor was that we had a common friend: JoDee! Gail grew up with her on Anderson Island. The world is quite tiny at times and filled with God's surprises!

Gail was riding with her soon to be husband, Jim and getting quite good at riding. She even rode to Sturgis in South Dakota and dealt with an emergency like a man; she towed Jim's bike and trailer with her bike for 20 miles. What a gal!

A Plan For You

I could visualize Gail and I being best friends as kids. We'd shake up the neighborhood on our bicycles.

Gail and I would laugh, celebrate, cry, scream, vent and look for answers to life's storms that kept coming our way. Another thing that we had in common was we agreed there was a God reason to everything that happened or didn't.

But before the storms that were about to hit me hard, a big miracle was to be celebrated May 2005.

One Warm afternoon I was walking with Gail and my Activity Director at lunch time. I knew the time was getting close for delivery of *Time To Come Home*, so I left a note on my door for the delivery driver.

When I received the call on my cell phone from the driver, I literally shrilled: "They're here; oh my God, they're here!" My adrenalin went into seventh gear. "I gotta' go - I gotta' go!" Gail said, "I get the first copy!"

"Okay," I yelled back, as I ran back to the facility and rode home.

I wasn't even prepared for what occurred next: I praised God over and over as I brought all of the boxes - 1,000 copies of *Time* into the house. I sat in my chair to rest from all of the rushing that was flushing through my veins, pumping me up passed the point of joy when a strong wave of anxiety took over, drowning out that exhilarating moment. Satan messed with my head as negative thoughts oozed out of my mouth. "Oh Lord, this book is filled with many secrets and truths of what a bad lady I used to be. I can't share this book with anyone; I just can't do it." I was concerned about what was in the contents of this book that I had dedicated to God, as promised Him back in 1989.

The few people who had read it responded with: "Wows," and even the editors said they enjoyed it, couldn't stop reading it, and made unbelievable comments, even wanted to meet me.

"I sacrificed myself to tell these things, Lord."

"Jesus sacrificed His life for yours!" came piercing right back at me.

Testimonies aren't all about warm and fuzzy feelings; they are often about harsh reality. Sharing the glory of God isn't as affective without a battle, struggle or sacrifice to come through.

And so *Time To Come Home* went out to the public library, and to family and friends who know me. Although shocking information was revealed; the responses were electrocuting. The readers liked the story, thought it was well written, related in some way, couldn't stop reading it and said what a survivor I was to go through all of that, and so on ... I was even called anointed and appointed by pastors. Praise God!

The story is a strongly told but a humbling one. My head is intact, but my heart wants to see my writing distributed past people who know me. I know this will transpire, as I kept my promise to God and He always keeps His promises – always!

Philippians 3:14 - *"I press on toward the goal to win the prize which God has called me heavenward in Christ Jesus!"*

Stormy's Storm

Chapter 38

My sister Stormy and her husband Danny had been together for more than 20 years. They knew each other in junior high, but didn't get together until after her divorce. They rode a Harley-Davidson and did the two-step together. Danny used to teach this country dance. He was a cowboy/biker. Danny had many friends, most from the biker world. He took a strong liking to Stormy's family and friends, and to him anyone in his life was **family**.

Danny told his family and friends that when he and Stormy first got together, he was impressed by how tough she was. When she came to visit him, he was surprised by her response to his pet pit bull and rattle snake. As they were getting ready to go into the house, he warned her and she responded, "So blanking' what!" The dog loved her and so did Danny.

Danny put up with her mean episodes, which came when she drank too much. He'd go to a motel or to a friend's place for the night until she sobered up. He never lay a hand on her, even when she swung her fists at him. Yes, an inherited Dad gene of violence remained in Sister, Stormy and Sherry, as well. Their life style was different and destructive in my eyes. I never criticized them although I disagreed with how they lived. My sisters love me the best they know how, but they have called me, "Jesus Freak!" A name I'm quite proud to take. I recall a year prior to Danny dying, riding in a car with my sisters, and Stormy said, "A lot of our friends are dead, or they are born again Christians," and she laughed; then turned to me and apologized.

> Jesus said, in *Matthew 5:11 - Blessed are you when people insult you, persecute you, say all kinds of evil against you because of me. Rejoice and be glad because great is your reward in heaven.*

I turn the other cheek and love them like Jesus, and that means don't act Holier than Thou. Jesus doesn't want to be pushed down people's throats. That's not His way. His yoke is easy, and His burden is light. He loves you like you are the only person in the world! A personal relationship is what he desires of people. He desires a person to come to him of their own choosing.

I pray for my sisters' salvation the same as I do for my son's. Daddy Frank invested many prayers for the sisters, brother, son- in-laws and grandchildren; their salvation had high priority with him!

A Plan For You

Stormy and Danny partied hard, which would catch up with Danny. They went to the Redwood Run every year for 17 years. Danny was known as the Mayor of this yearly event. During this event heavy drinking and other unhealthy activities occurred. The kind of partying that can bring people to their early grave.

A few days had past since the Run; Stormy and Danny were celebrating Sherry's Birthday at Mom and Daddy's house. Danny complained he wasn't feeling well and told Stormy to stay and enjoy herself while he went home to lie down.

When Stormy came home she found Danny lying on the floor, he was blue and his face was in vomit. He was still talking, but not much. He had suffered a stroke. Danny was taken to the hospital where he had a heart attack, and then open heart surgery and his body gave out.

Danny was only 51 years old, and the partying was evident to the doctors. But they did everything under their power to save him.

Stormy came unglued. She was grief –stricken. She didn't know Jesus and now she hated Him for taking Danny away from her. Without Jesus, this kind of thinking and bitterness only leads to destructive life patterns, which was already a way of life for Stormy. Daddy Frank, Mom and I prayed this would open Stormy's eyes to what this life style does to a person, but she wanted to die and go be with him. She no longer cared if she lived. Just the way my friend Cindy felt when her husband died.

A Plan For You

Danny did enjoy the country gospel music, mom always played when he and Stormy visited. He knew where Mom and Daddy stood with Jesus, the whole family knew. So hopefully at least one seed was planted and Danny accepted Jesus. We never know what people do on their death bed. We can only pray they are given one last chance.

I had a dream about Danny shortly after he died:

Danny, Gail and I were riding our motorcycles. We stopped at a few parties, but Danny didn't want to stay, he seemed to be on a mission. We picked Stormy up at one of the parties. She kept trying to get him to stop to party, but he looked straight ahead and Gail and I followed closely behind. The surroundings became beautiful; it was bright, brighter than sun light. The temperature was perfect. There were vivid green grassy mountains and the aqua ocean was along side of the road we were traveling. It was as though Danny had tunnel vision and I suddenly realized where we were heading: Jerusalem!

Only the spiritually connected can comprehend the significance of this dream. It is sad that Stormy chose to be bitter and not accept Jesus as her Savior, because this dream would bring her peace. I know Jesus is knocking on her heart.

Jerusalem has high priority to God. The Bible is filled with versus that indicate as much, too many versus for me to write down. But I want to share another dream that reveals the importance of Jerusalem:

I was in a two story house. I was on the highest level. Lying in the bed, I turned my head to see the open window. I was compelled to go look out. There was a city in the sky, so close I could jump into it. The city sat on the fluffy white clouds and the roof tops were all pure gold. "It's heaven!" I said to myself out loud. "'If I jump out the window I can be there.'" But God did not want me to come yet and I woke up. The place I saw was the new Jerusalem.

Revelation 21: Then I saw a new heaven and a new earth, for the first heaven and the first earth had passed away, and there was no more sea. I saw the Holy City, the new Jerusalem coming down out of heaven from God, prepared as a bride beautifully dressed for her husband.

Stormy still grieves and I know she hopes there's a Jesus and a heaven. I only pray it's enough hope to bring her into the arms of Jesus, so that His true power of healing can take place. He yearns to love and hold her. May she embrace His undying love for her!

Memory Lane

Chapter 39

Danny's memorial was a huge event, mostly bikers attended. I will never forget the agony on Stormy's soak and wet face when she started Danny's bike. Standing next to me at that moment was my purple Cadillac convertible friend, Shannon. We talked about her sister Bobbie and how she used to live just like Stormy and Danny. And when she looked at Stormy it made her think of Bobbie.

For those who read *Time to Come Home* Bobbie, her husband and four year old daughter were murdered by their hired hand.

Shannon's other sister married one of my cousins so we always felt this officially made us family.

Shannon and I kept in touch through the years, but this moment was a rekindling of our family connectedness. She had read *Time* and was awe stricken by it; she said that I should have a movie made. I laughed and said," Who's gonna' play my Dad?"

A Plan For You

We talked about our purple Cadillac rides on the boardwalk strip; we remembered Bobbie and Marcie together; we talked about our trials and tragedies that we got through.

Her husband, Bill lost his arm in an accident around the same time Bobbie and her family was murdered and when Marcie had died; one of their triplets died; Bill's daughter that Shannon helped to raise was murdered shortly after she married - she was shot by an obsessed ex-boyfriend.

Their strength to hold up through these tragedies stems from their strong faith in Jesus. I am amazed by Shannon's strength and she is amazed by mine. We have sustaining faith!

I had a blessed opportunity in early spring of this year to spend some quality time with Shannon and Bill in their country home near Yosemite National Park. I had a refreshing and restful time, and saw a section of California I hadn't seen before.

There is a significant point to every person God has carefully placed in my life. I don't doubt this, but there are some people I would have preferred to have by passed altogether, but then my testimony wouldn't have been as audacious.

Shannon most obviously plays an important role in my life and me hers. I am thankful for our family connectedness in flesh and in spirit.

Daddy Frank

He came into our lives by way of a turquoise and white '55 Chevy, looking as handsome as movie star.
He drove without his hands on the wheel because he had to talk with his hands.
He was physically strong, carrying monster size garbage drums on his back for days and years. He was the hardest worker I knew, he could run circles around the younger men.
He believed in taking care of mom, showering her with romantic gifts, and providing for her four unruly children. He was the best example of a husband and a father.
He deserves an award beyond awards, and I know that he is receiving it first – hand from Jesus.
He brought fun into our lives. I remember him dancing like Elvis and playing the werewolf, chasing us through the house. He made popcorn that was better than movie popcorn. I remember the camping trips; he watered skied and couldn't even swim. And he was a Navy man. Yes, he was brave. He loved to fish and hunt, and he'd fry the whole fish and eat the head and all, he ate some pretty strange things. We will miss the stories about the big one that got away.

He was the most generous man I knew. He would literally give the shirt off of his back to his family, friends and church. He was loyal to his church, but most of all he was loyal to God. He loved the Lord with all of his heart and he earnestly prayed for his family and friends to do the same. He is still praying for us now; he's praying with Jesus. And he's breathing in eternal life!
We will miss him!
I love you Daddy Frank!

Love, Deena
Daddy went home to be with the Lord December 10, 2005.

What a Man

Chapter 40

Danny had only been gone for six months when Daddy's struggle to breathe intensified. He was on oxygen and gave himself inhalation therapy treatments several times a day.

Not that there was a contest, but we thought Mom would be the first to go, as she had been in and out of the hospital, close to her death bed, several times. And for Danny and Mark to die before the both of them was unexpected. And Marcie was the most unexpected death of all.

The doctors didn't give Daddy much time to live. Not only did he have emphazema, he had a bad heart. Mom wanted us to have a family reunion before he'd go home to Jesus. So May 2005, all eleven of us were together: Daddy, Mom, Me, Jim, Shayla, Sherry, Stormy, Danny, Chris, Shyla, and Shain.

The year 2006 would take two more lives from the family tree: Danny and Daddy.

I will never forget the day he drove in our driveway in his Chevy and how excited I was to meet him. And for him to be chosen by God to be the Dad of four unruly kids was a miracle. As mentioned, he was my hero and remains so to this day.

He was able to read *Time To Come Home* and see my Dedication to his titling the book. He was proud of me for my dedication to God and my accomplishments of going to college and of writing a book. It's not cheap publishing a book and he assisted me with the finances of getting it published. He was pleased with me and I was assured of this fact. Talking about Jesus with him was satisfying; his faith was bold and I guess one might say so was mine. Through the grapevine of family we knew we were lilies among the poppies. Yes, the family had a certain amount of respect for his faith, knew where he stood, but fully understanding where he was coming from can only be known by the dwelling of the Holy Spirit and it dwelled in Daddy and me.

He was at the stage of illness where going in and out of the hospital was becoming an unwelcome occurrence. Mom knew exactly what this felt like and was sympathetic. She was also scared as the obvious of him nearing death was evident.

We talked about her fears and struggles with Daddy's severe illness and how it was impacting her and him. I may have been a long distance away, but I was there with her and Daddy in heart. My Mom found strength in my faith. She was not as strong as Daddy and I were. But she was a believer, and was now the encourager of Daddy as his illness was severely depressing him. Being the strong man that he had been most of his life, made it hard for him to accept or deal with his disabilities. He was a faithful fighter.

But he was losing the fight. God was calling him home. Mom knew first-hand how to deal with sickness that debilitated, as she had lots of unwanted visits in the hospital for her illnesses.

I never knew whether I should visit Daddy in the hospital to say goodbye. Like when Mom went in and out of the hospital, I didn't know whether to fly down to see her or wait for her funeral and fly there again. It's not a cheap deal to fly or to drive 1,000 miles. So as sad as that statement sounds, it was and still is a harsh reality, as Mom still goes in and out of the hospital. She laughs and says, "I needed a vacation so I came to the hospital to rest."

Mom's health is very fragile. Every one that knows her is aware that she has a serious drinking problem and her liver is shot, and maybe her kidneys are affected as she is diabetic as well. She has been sober for several months as of to date. No matter that some of mom's illnesses are self- inflicted, she is my Mother and I love her with all my heart. I'm not going to prosecute her for her weakness. I pray for healing of her body, mind and spirit. Jesus can do it, if she'd give it all to Him. I will keep on loving her even if she fails again. That's how Jesus loves us. That would be like saying Daddy smoked and caused his health problems, "so too bad so sad that's what he gets."

If we condemn others and stop loving and caring for them because they fowled up, then we'd better

A Plan For You

point a bigger accusing finger at our own self. We all fall short of the glory of God and are sinners. By God's grace we are saved and not because we're better than someone else or think we're holier than thou. Here's a commandment to seriously consider: Love them like Jesus!

Daddy knew all about the love of Jesus. I was able to say my goodbye to Daddy by phone. I told him how much I loved him and he responded, "I love you, too; you know the love of Jesus, real love. The others say they love me, but they don't know real love." And even in his dying days, I don't doubt that he prayed the rest of the family would accept Jesus and know real love.

When I got the call that he had died, I was driving in my truck. I was shocked. I guess it doesn't matter that you know end of life is approaching, it still is a gut wrenching: "Ahhhh, no, it isn't true" when the message first hits home. Then the tears came pouring out like there was a water fountain in back of my eyes, and the loud uncontrolled bawling. I had to pull off of the road. What do I do without Daddy?

His funeral was quite the send off to heaven. He had three pastors talk about him; he was good friends with all of them. We laughed at the funny stories they recalled about Daddy's character. Like the one pastor Ted shared: "There were two things that Frank never did: wear his seat belt or use the emergency brake." Ted was going to drive Dad and Mom to a doctor appointment in Mom's Cadillac. When Ted attempted to pull out of the garage, neither Ted nor Dad could figure out how to release the emergency button. Daddy had driven the Caddy for many years, and apparently never used this brake, nor did he pay attention to the fact it was automatic. Mom waited in the driveway, wondering what was taking so long. Daddy grumbled as they tried to figure out where the release button was. Finally Ted put the car in reverse, "poof," the brake was released. Mom was standing along side of the driveway waiting for them to get out of the garage. Family and friends were roaring with laughter.

I watched my son go to his casket and touch his chest and hand. He said something to him: probably:"I love you, Grandpa." I knew he was Jim's hero as well.

He admired how he worked hard to provide for his family, and was always ready to lend a helping hand to his family and friends. He was a generous man; unfortunately sometimes his generosity was taken advantage of, but this never stopped him from giving. He would have literally given the shirt of his back to help someone else.

I can't get into my son's mind, but I do know he admired and would miss his Grandpa. He wanted to be most like him when he grew up and in many ways this happened. I'm thankful that Jim had Daddy Frank for an example. He knew right where Grandpa stood with Jesus.

Daddy told me that he would be 33 years old when he went to heaven; that he thought everyone would be this age, as Jesus was 33 years old when he resurrected and went to heaven. I don't know how factual this thought is, but I do know Daddy is 33 years old today, and he's with Marcie, Mark and hopefully Danny – may enough of a Jesus seed have been placed in his heart and in all of the hearts of his children – Amen!

We were blest to have Daddy Frank in our lives for 46 years. Mom and he had their 44th anniversary one month prior to his death.

Mom dealt with her grief by taking up writing. She wrote poems and short stories. I knew Mom enjoyed reading and was an avid reader, but I didn't know she could write. It looks as though I followed in her foot steps. So I shall end this chapter with her poem about Daddy.

"I love you all dearly
Now don't shed a tear
I'm spending my Christmas
with Jesus this year."
We miss you!
We miss you most at Christmas
You were like a little kid.
You always loved a good surprise,
and now were glad you did.
You loved to have family near,
sometimes it was more than family,
but you did not care.
It was always your job to carve the meat,
of course you had to taste it,
and lick your fingers to make sure
it was good enough to eat.
When everyone sat down and found their place,
They were all silent
until you said grace.

By Millie Cardinale
My Mom

Back at the Ranch

Chapter 41

Meanwhile back at the ranch (the home front), I struggled to deal with the Manager Position and going back and forth to Santa Cruz for funerals. I never wanted to be the Activity Manager, but Michelle, my prior Director, insisted I'd be perfect for the position. She was moving on. I already knew what a hard pressing, stressed out position it would be. I had avoided this job at my two previous work places, as stress and me shouldn't engage. It's like living close to a heart explosion because of my strong need to over-achieve. As read in previous chapters, I am an over- achiever. So I gotta' prove I can do it. It meant more money, but way more responsibility and tension; more than a high strung individual like me should be messing with.

Gail and Cindy helped me through my pain, by listening to me. Cindy had a true understanding of what Stormy was going through, and Gail had lost her Dad and she was very close to him.

A Plan For You

I needed to talk about the tragedies in my life, but I couldn't go deep about it, as I wasn't going to let my weak self show up. I had to be tough so if I started to cry, I quickly shut it off. Both friends were concerned for my well-being. I would tell myself I can't do this crying thing now I got to perform my job duties, which required more of me than I could endure. I was using my work to escape thinking at all. However, the time bomb was getting ready to blow.

I worked way beyond the norm to be successful at my job. I give myself credit for being a smart, skilled and a multi-talented woman, but dang, life's hard knocks were overwhelming. I had chest pains, anxiety spells, and I worked from home to keep up with the job. Put conscientious and grief-stricken together and what do you have – suicide. But I kept going by reminding myself that I had dealt with the biggest grief ever - Marcie's death, as if that gave me some logic to escape grieving over Daddy.

I was getting to a non-functioning point. I slept all weekend and I had no energy for book writing. It was that lifeless syndrome hitting hard, in other words: DEEP DEPRESSION. I had to do whatever it took to perform my job and not think about the deep sadness that surrounded me. I tried to comfort Mom who was suffering. But I was dealing with my own grief (by avoiding it). I don't know that I was much comfort to her, but I did my best.

I had another book to work on, **this book**. Writing is the big part of the plan that the Lord has me in the world to do for Him. But grieving is a necessary process to bring healing to the soul. And God wanted me to let my tears go up to him, so He could comfort me.

I sat in my easy chair that I was going to go to *Barnes and Noble* to buy back in 2003 (see previous chapter). It was February 2006. I could barely pray. I was so worn down to the depths of numbness, but I could feel the pain rising forth. Then a shot of reality slapped me in the face so hard the bottled up pain shattered, making a loud noise: I screamed out a cry that was reaching heaven. "I'm so tired, Lord. I miss my Daddy so much! How do I go on without him? My job is killing me. Life really sucks right now. Please help me!"

God placed answers in my heart that would restore my strength and bring me back to the talent of writing. Writing is one of God's ways to help me get through grief, as well as crying my guts out. So the answer came in the midst of my agony:

I went to work the next day and talked to my boss. I told him I wanted to step down from the Manager position and go back to the job of Activity Director for the Alzheimer's/Dementia Unit; that I was content doing this and it left me time to write on my next book. I needed the mental balance. He was accommodating and gracious about it and told me I did a good job as Manager. He gave me back my previous job as Director of the unit. My energy was eventually restored; therefore my smile and laughter gave out reflections from the light of Jesus. My mom once told me my best features were my smile and my laughter. And when my heart doesn't hurt, I think she's right.

Our new Activity Manager, Connie was great to work along side of. We had mutual respect and accented one another with our talents and skills. Although she was my Manager, she stayed next to me and didn't feel the need to rise above me. She had a calm demeanor which complemented my high strung nature. Like Michelle, I felt right at home with Connie. I was appreciated and respected for my abilities and who I was by both of them. Connie was impressed by my first book and couldn't wait for this one to be published. She was in support of my dream.

I was content and moving along on my writing, the balance was good. Without the pressure, I could love on the residents and truly enjoy my job, and serve my Savior with a smile in my healed heart.

Reflection

How can it be -
that I am a reflection of thee?
They see you in my smile, my touch my song
How can it be -
that I am a reflection of thee?
They see you in my walk, my words,
my heart,
How can it be -
that I am a reflection of thee?

This poem is written to honor my faithful friends in Jesus who serve the residents with me: Marie, Shawn, Betty and John and all of the other spiritual volunteers that are affiliated with them. Thank You!

Friends in Jesus

Chapter 42

Marie

Marie has been serving the residents where I work for many years. I enjoy her English accent. She has a sincere and soft nature about her; yet she's a fervent prayer warrior for the residents. I saw the heart of Jesus in her right away. I have known her for nearly four years. She and other church members make my Sundays as special as the residents'. I attend church at work. I make sure everyone gets to church on time and that's a big job, but I am glad to do it! Marie has prayed me through my troubled waters, putting her own pains and problems aside to do so; that's how she is for all those she prays for. She genuinely cares for the hearts of others. She has a compassionate heart – just like Jesus!

Shawn

Shawn is a gentle giant for Jesus. He's a tall nurse with a healthy structure –He over towers most of the more than 100 staff members, not to mention the residents. He is studying to be a missionary and he knows how to fly aircraft; which can be an asset in the mission field. He's quiet and shy until you get to know him. And I got to know him, as God had a plan for his knowledge in computers to assist me in His plan to publicize *Time To come Home* on the internet. Shawn was unselfishly willing to accommodate me. Jesus knows what he's doing every step of the way, as he walks along side of those who accept Him and love Him. He unites people to carry out His will. And I'd like to thank Shawn for being a good servant for Jesus and a friend to me.

Betty

Betty is a beautiful African American; her eyes are big and round and almost black. I met Betty three years ago. She is my age and we had similar backgrounds – meaning sinful pasts, bad girls and all. We probably would have been the pair to avoid in our immature younger years. We laugh at some of our past experiences as we can, because we know we are free in Jesus today.

Betty is a Chaplain for nursing homes. Not only am I blessed to attend service every Sunday but also on Wednesdays with Betty. I get the best of both worlds: Worship Services and friends in Jesus.

Betty calls the Alzheimer's Unit "God's Joy Group." They are a special group – but I am bias, as I am the Activity Director for these unique people. Betty radiates Jesus and when she first met me she said the same about me. It is a wonderful experience to put the radiation together.

She has been a confidant and a friend who has helped me stand up against the enemy who was coming after me through other people in the work place. Betty is another big blessing in God's plan for me.

Johnny Blaze

Where do I begin about John? He has long dark hair, brown eyes and he wears biker attire; he's nice looking, if rough and rugged is a look you go for. And we already know I like this look. When I'm not working, I have a whole other wild and ready for the wind look myself.

John is loud and hyper and makes no excuses for his character. He's certain that Jesus loves him and is assured that He loves everyone and attests to this fact, as he knows what Jesus brought him out of. He was a big time drug user/alcoholic – you name it, he did it. He spent time in prison – he says he earned the title: *Peckerwood* (for more details look it up on the internet or talk to someone in prison). He wants people who struggle the way he did, to know if God can save him, he can save anybody. He was about as lost and far from God as a person could get.

He told me how his mother used to pray for his salvation all the time, even in the midst of his highs and drunkenness, which were almost always. She continued to pray for him. She was a faithful believer.

His mother died before she saw her son commit his life to Jesus; although, she is fully aware of this fact, as she has visited him from heaven and prayed over him to release a demon that had a hold on him.

John said when he gave his life to Jesus; he gave Him all of his addictions and bad habits: drugs, alcohol, cigarettes and cussing, too. When he hit rock bottom, which seems to be a place so many of us get before we give our lives to Jesus, he knew he was making a choice to live, because death was so close it was anticipating snuffing him out; in other words, Satan was waiting to bring him to hell. But God!

God's elite are uniquely designed and come from every walk of life. He chose his elite before the foundations of the earth. He knew we were going to come to Him, serve Him, and we'd be on our knees and have our faces on the floor when we came home.

John boldly brags about what God has done for him. He has committed his life to Jesus. Picture this young wild looking guy riding to a nursing home on a Harley-Davidson, carrying his Bible in the facility with him. He studies the Bible with the residents, and sets up church for them on another evening. He's dedicated to this ministry.

After getting to know this unique man, I am amazed that he would minister to a bunch of old sick people. And they look forward to seeing him and worshipping the Lord with him. I admired him. Perhaps too much – no it was too much.

John and I became riding buddies. When he got his bike, he knew that I was a Christian and rode a motorcycle for Jesus. He read my *Time* book, and learned we had some similar experiences and that we had some bad ass dads. He reminded me of my brother in many ways. We talked on the phone every day; we rode once or twice a week; and we ate meals and watched movies together. We were getting to know one another on a deep level. I never had a man friend I could be so open with; I told him things no other people know. I trusted him. It was easy; the man was all about Jesus.

I am 11 years older than John and I don't think anyone can tell. I'm not an old looking woman. Despite how my Dad reminded me that I was ugly and slapped me for being ugly, I'm not so bad to look at. I was attracted to John, but was able to keep things healthy. But as time moved on the attraction was getting out of control with me. I got all confused and wanted God's perspective. I thought God put us together as we have common interests, so maybe it was suppose to be more? I was also dealing with a stressed out situation at work, one of those killer type stresses (see next chapter). I was vulnerable and my heart was filled with human – fleshly confusion. I pushed John away at first, because I felt it was the best thing to do; then I hated not hearing from him and he wanted to do the adult thing (which was a healthy response) so he wouldn't talk to me.

A Plan For You

I felt as though I had a breakdown of some sort, because I went out of control and I didn't care what I did or said or if God cared. Somebody had to pay for all this anger, pain and confusion, so I called the man at least seven times and left messages on his recorder, begging him to talk to me. Then a whole night went by and I totally went mad. I left him a lovely message on his message machine. "I love you like a brother in Christ, but I am mad at myself for ever sharing any of my secrets with you, and I won't EVER make that mistake again with anyone. And you need to take responsibility for your part in this!"

I hadn't seen this side of me in years. At first it felt good to be angry; that way I was able to bury some of the pain by telling myself it was okay to be mad about all that was going on: My best friend wouldn't talk to me and my new young boss was attempting to remove me from my job.

I felt insignificant, and that's an understatement.

I prayed as much as I could muster up: "Just get me through another day, Jesus!"

My faith was floating in deep and dangerous waters, as my Jesus light grew dim, I knew by faith that He was carrying me through; although I couldn't feel His presence in the air or anywhere. There was nothing left to do but be still and let God. When I submitted my silent self to Him, the answers came rolling in.

I had to be separated from John in order to hear God's quiet still voice, and so I could see clearly what he wanted to do about us. We don't talk anymore, but for an occasional call on a message recorder, or my

A Plan For You

one-sided emails, I know that Jesus intends to renew our friendship His way. And as John always says, "Father, we thank you for what you're going to do in our lives."

My friend Betty pointed out to me that God wants my total focus and it's obvious I wasn't totally focused on Him. She went on to say what I already knew, "God is a Jealous God." I had to ask for His forgiveness. I was relieved, as that was a firm reminder of how important my life and full attention is to Him.

Totally

I am totally into you, my Lord, Jesus!
My whole life, my everything is about
your life;
I exist for you.
I know that I know, that thou art God!
Being your elite has repercussions;
I tripped and fell into my fleshly being,
my spiritual self choked.
Satan smothered me with obsession,
confusion and anger;
My flesh was raging out of control.
I misunderstood a young man's friendship,
his wonderful spiritual friendship.
I smeared it up until I could no longer
identify myself in you.
Oh God, my Lord and Savior,
I am totally into you,
My whole life, my everything is
about your life;
I exist for you.
I know that I know that Thou art God!
Being your elite comes with your promises;
I tripped and fell and you caught me,
you brought me to my spiritual senses;
Your healing hands will mend the friendship
that is in your tender care.
You will raise me up and strengthen me,
As I am your spiritual being,
And I am totally into you
my Lord, Jesus!
Praise you!

Power Hungry Heads

Chapter 43

Connie moved to another department. My security and satisfaction with my job was just about to be uprooted like a giant weed and then poison sprayed on it to keep it from sprouting back. We picked another Director together even though Jane said I didn't pick her; I had everything to do with her being hired. She was young and had no Manager experience. She said she was glad to work with me so she could learn from me. She seemed to have respect for my 23 years experience in this field. I felt good about teaching what I knew. Jane was excited and eager for the position. We worked well together for about one month.

I watched her change into a power hungry person. She seemed to believe her position gave her the right to snap at people. I watched her sharp tongue some aides and then I saw her bully Mo. Mo had been with the facility for 14 years. She was a dynamo woman. She could run circles around many young people.

A Plan For You

Mo was 88 years old, and looked 60 years old. She had a super big heart for the residents. She didn't like paper work, but she loved being with the people, and went out of her way to do unique and special things for them. She was struggling with some health issues and needed a leave of absence. The new head boss was looking to get Mo to retire; but I don't feel she was going about it in the right way; political crap games is the real name for what she and Jane were doing to Mo.

And when I saw how Jane raised her voice and barked at Mo, I was sick to my stomach. At that moment I knew Connie and I had made a mistake, but I was going to have to deal with it. Mo was gone and the next person in line was about to get her dose of the power monster Jane had become.

Then I watched the newest woman bullied and lied about to get her out. This gal found another job after she dealt with mental repercussions from being treated like a bad little child.

And then there's me; of course she came after me. I had the most power to drown out. I didn't agree with the way she managed, nor did I like her last minute ways of doing things. She wrote me up twice; the second time she was quite clever in how she made it look like her failure was my problem. I was made to look like a trouble maker for talking to the newest boss and not going to her first. And then he didn't support me. He said she had the right to do what she did in so many words - not very reassuring.

I felt defeated and worn out. I kept going to work in spite of the fact I didn't like this woman and she

A Plan For You

really didn't know what she was doing. I asked Jesus to get me away from her, from this workplace. God calls us to forgive and pray for those who offend us, so as hard as it was squeeze out kind words, I'd do it. I was faithful about praying. I was in such a bad mental way, I was obsessed about how to get revenge; no, how to forgive her; no, how to get rid of her, no, how to do what God wanted me to; no, how to ...

As I've mentioned before, Jesus knows what it feels like to be wrongly accused and I do too. It's a crippling experience.

So my friends Betty, Marie and John prayed with me and for me. And other friends tried to reassure and keep me going. I have this remarkable way to endure pressure and pain. I think I'm weak and I can't go on, yet I keep on moving even when I can't feel my body anymore. My friends tell me I am strong, even when I feel like I'm falling apart.

I had a lot of praying to do to get to the point of forgiving, but I did it. God made it obvious that Jane did not know what she was doing. I said back to God, "So if this is the case, then move her out of the job." But building my character would take more time with Jane. I obeyed God, even when I didn't always want to in this case.

With time, we could work together; I would ignore what bothered me so I could stay getting along. I made her a birthday card and I took her out to lunch – wow, what an accomplishment.

February 2008 Jane was leaving to go to school, and I wrote her another card wishing her well and to take Jesus with her when she goes – because that's the only way to succeed in life! Before she left she gave me an excellent evaluation. And that's the favor of God!

Power Hungry, Too

Our new Director came with very little experience as a Manager. She had a kind demeanor and she was willing to work with Lilly and I. She promised she wouldn't be like Jane. She had been working as an assistant with us and when the position opened she begged me to take it and said she'd help me. We already know why I said, "No way."

I explained to Linda that I would help her if she got the job; Lilly agreed that she would as well. We both worked more years in the activity field than Linda.

Linda was good at planning, organizing and facilitating programs. She was a hard worker and willing to go the extra mile to be affective. Although this was a similar situation as the last Director, Linda was different and had a sweeter disposition. She was receptive of my training and told all the other Managers that she didn't know what she'd do without me. I was relaxed about my job again. I felt important. I thanked God and prayed for a peaceful working team and environment. I am all about peace. My other prayer has been to be a successful writer for Jesus and moved out of this work. However, I enjoy many aspects of my job, and could be content if respected and left alone to do my job.

A Plan For You

A month in the door seems to be the magic number for these young Managers to get a sense of power and then not know what to do with it. I watched Linda go for Lilly.

At first she was writing her out a minute by minute schedule to follow. Lilly tried to stay still although she felt demeaned. Then she followed Lilly around and found fault with her, even when Lilly was doing her job. When Lilly tried to explain, Linda would not listen. Well, need I say much more: the poor treatment appeared intentional and in my eyes was getting out of hand? Linda wrote Lilly up for not communicating and when Lilly tried to communicate, Linda would interrupt and not listen. Lilly tried her best not to fight, but eventually there were some loud confrontations, and the big boss was pulled in, and basically told Lilly to deal with what I could see wasn't fair treatment, or he'd have to ask her to leave. But he never asked me what was going on. I am filled with insight and awareness to truths about mismanaging going on in the department - had been experiencing a whole lot of it lately. So far Linda was still treating me well.

I came into work on a Sunday morning to find Lilly's desk cleared. I knew what had happened and asked God to get me away from this place. I was sad, because Lilly was my friend and I had known her for seven years. I had taught her my job at a prior facility. And then Connie and I trained her together for this position. Lilly groomed herself; she was a beautiful Pilipino. Not only was she all about beautifying herself, she did the same for the residents. She was

A Plan For You

a hard worker and the residents appreciated this beautiful woman.

I didn't feel her firing was just. I was watching all the negative Management, as I was one of the star victims in this live stage play.

I don't know exactly know Linda's motive when the same treatment was directed at me. Oh boy, here I go again. She questioned what I did all day? I felt insulted by this question so I responded," I sit on my butt all day and do nothing." Then she was going to try and change my schedule around and pretty much control me like a puppet - that's my analysis.

Stop right now, Linda; I'm quitting."

"GOOD! When?"

"Two weeks," I answered.

"GOOD!"

She went straight to the bosses' office and told him what had happened in her way, by leaving out the "Good's." She told him she didn't want me to leave and wanted him to ask me to stay.

I told him I don't work well with people needing to control me; he said he understood and asked me to stay and I did so.

But Linda didn't treat me any better. She reminded me sharply the she was my Director and would tell me what to do.

Now how do you think I wanted to respond to that statement; I wanted to beat the crap out of her. But being God's girl I had to grit my teeth and say, "Okay, I understand."

Then I was intentionally reprimanded in front of people in group settings; things that I wasn't at fault for doing, just so she could throw her weight around. I knew she wanted me gone, as I was a threat to her. And if I could have been gone I would have been most delighted.

Gail kept me hanging in there at the job; the prayers of faithful friends were helping me; although I felt like hiding from life, instead of dealing with all this injustice.

It ain't the first time I've been a walking wounded zombie. I went to the doctor who gave me two weeks off for mental health reasons.

When I returned, Linda had decided to make big changes that would upset me and some of the Managers. No rest for the weary. She had removed me from being in charge of the Special Care Unit. She shuffled me around like a pee on – the power thing. I wanted to get out more than ever, but the Managers begged me to stay. I didn't even have to say anything to them, as they were aware of what was happening; Linda was self- destructing. The residents that had the mental capacity to be aware were not pleased with my not being with them. I told them in a kind and professional way that we were just going to make changes so that they could get to know the other Activity staff. Family members were upset. And of course, I was blamed for making trouble.

Of course, I'm saying, "Why God? Where do these controlling people come from?" I'm not against being directed, but to be controlled is a big issue. I'll fight it when it is unjust as can be read in former chapters.

Linda argued with some of the Mangers and the next thing I knew she was apologizing to them and me. She sounded so sincere; she hugged me and admitted that she was wrong in the way she had treated me. I forgave her! And the Unit is mine once again. The bumpy rides in the past two years have been hard enough to say there's a happy ending. I'm merely thankful for the peace between Linda and I.

I don't have all the answers to why I had to go through this twice and deal with so much down sizing of character and spiritual unrest, but Satan has no hold on me because God prevails **Every Time** and **All the Time.**

I assume my lesson in all this is forgiveness, endurance, patience, believing, trusting, and knowing that I am God's girl and He's got me covered **All the Time**.

Go Ahead

Go ahead and cry – let the tears flow
Every cheek rolling drop reaches Jesus
His Word promises and is clear
He catches every glistening bead
in – place in His nail scared hand
and places it a carefully crafted bottle
So let the rain fall
for after the storm
comes tears of joy and laughter
Each healing drop is counted by our Lord
He cares this much about our individual
pain and our joy –
Joy always returns for those who
love and trust in Jesus!
So go ahead …

Care Givers and Earth Angels

Chapter 44

This is a good time to write something about the blessed work the Caregivers and I do for Jesus, and to say something more about the special people we work with!

Caregivers are among the wealthiest people in the world. And many may not be aware of this fact.

A Caregiver's job can be mentally and physically challenging, as they spend most of their waking hours caring for the sick, disabled, demented and mentally ill. Their job is not a walk in the park; sometimes it can be more like walking in a land mine.

Yes, the Caregiver's job has its rewards: the smiles, the hugs, the healing – does the heart good! And their heart is reaping in more than they can fathom.

The Caregiver is of God's favor. They were appointed for this special service by Him. Their blessings aren't of material wealth, but of spiritual wealth, which is a far better blessing!

Suppose God blest every one of His chosen children with material wealth. How then would He get Caregivers to work for Him? A Caregiver's work is reaping unbelievable blessings here and now, but especially in His Kingdom!

So my fellow Caregivers, know that your mission hear on earth is reaching Heaven and the heart of God!

Earth Angels

*There's a group of people one would never
believe to be Earth Angels
They are confused with Dementia and
Alzheimer's, living other dimensions
of life that can bring frustrating
circumstances
In the midst of it all, those who care for
them learn to be patient, compassionate
and to love unconditionally
God is mysterious in His ways
And if we are to learn to love like Him
He will fill our hearts and lives with
Earth Angels
Like you wouldn't believe!*

God's Plan

Chapter 45

Okay, here's what readers have been anticipating: the magnificent miraculous ending.

God gives His children special gifts, and I have been blest to have several: the gift to put His words and messages in story form; the gift to serve the sick, disabled and demented; the gift to ride a motorcycle and be an example of His love among a not so easy group to minister to; a gift to be real and who I am in Jesus, no matter where I am and who I'm with; a gift to hold up under the toughest of times and still come out loving Jesus no matter what.

If a person looks at the gifts God has blest them with, one would be surprised how many they actually have. I'm sure I could list some more, but I have made my point: I am blest and assured of this fact.

My character is made stronger for what I have endured. Valleys in life build character. And I'm sure I have some more character building to come. I

A Plan For You

---

have been primed by my Lord to prepare me for my mission fields.

If you open your heart and eyes to Jesus, you will see that His Plan for your life is eternal life with Him. What's all the material prosperity going to bring; it's all temporary, but God is forever. That's where the real prosperity lies, and that's where I build my treasures.

I wrote two books waiting for some big hurkin' dream to transpire, and in all my hard efforts to reach the dream, my answer to God's plan is so ironic. I am tickled in my spirit when I realize what it is. I've been carefully chosen to play a significant role in sharing the love of Jesus in this world, and that's an awesome undertaking and realization. His Plan is the same for all of those who serve and follow Jesus.

God gives us unique characteristics and ways to share His profound message, which is **SALVATION**, and for people *to know Jesus and to make Him known*. What is greater than eternal life with Jesus – nothing. End of Story!

Philippians 1:6 - He that began a good work in you will bring it to completion until the day of Christ Jesus.

***

improve our intellectual capacity, learning, retain
optimizing our brain performance

amino acid
antioxide: A C E
  Berry b Beets
             Kale —   onion
  C   Spinach — red bell pepper
  antioxidant Garlic =
an protects our brain from free radical damage
our
retrain your taste board

HDL
LDL bad

4mg